Out of My

Out of My Mind

From flower power to the Third Millennium: the seventies, the eighties and the nineties

Richard Neville

BLOOMSBURY

To Julie

Thanks to Susan Haynes for starting it all off, years ago; to
Andrew Fisher for standing by, as always; to Jane Mills for
editorial input; and to Monica Macdonald at Bloomsbury for
fabulous faxing and devotion to duty. Since first publication,
have I polished and cut, embellished and fiddled? You bet.
Cyber correspondence welcome at rneville@ozemail.com.au

First published in Great Britain 1996
Bloomsbury Publishing Plc, 2 Soho Square, London W1V 6HB

ISBN 0 7475 2532 3

10 9 8 7 6 5 4 3 2 1

Typeset by Hewer Text Composition Services, Edinburgh
Printed in Great Britain by Clays Ltd, St Ives plc

Contents

Contents

Prologue:
Nowhere to Go

It should have been the best time of my life, but it wasn't. I was thirty, drained, self-conscious and baffled, having just won the longest obscenity trial in British history. Ideas and notions swirled in my head, but I didn't know which were my own and which were propaganda. My personal life was a mess, the public profile a millstone. In London, the counter-culture was falling apart, and so was I. Yet still I clambered on to the soapbox, insisting we were getting it all together . . .

What to do?

Disappear. I coaxed an assignment from the Evening Standard to report on the 1972 US Presidential campaign, but that was a front. I wanted to immerse myself in the culture of protest, to become re-inspired, to try to rekindle a flame that was failing.

The magazine I had founded had drifted to other hands, desperately trying to exploit the hype of the trial, and plunging ever downmarket. This piece was filed for Oz from afar, a kind of farewell I suppose, and nothing of which to be proud. But for the kind of journey this book represents, it is the proper place to begin.

1972:

It was dusk in Miami Beach as the crowd gathered outside the Albion Hotel. The Democratic Convention was over and the garbologist had come with a huge pink birthday cake. It was for Jerry Rubin, thirty-six years old this day, to be presented along with 'certificates of retirement from the Youth Movement' to himself and co-yippie founder Abbie Hoffman. The cake was inscribed: 'Never trust anyone over thirty.'

Milling in the forecourt were the park people, the zippies, formerly yippies. Through a portable amplifier, they raged about the yippies ripping off the Movement, losing touch with the kids in the streets and how people who live in penthouses shouldn't get stoned.

In retaliation, yippie celebs splashed water from their overlooking bedrooms and sent down their bodyguards.

A. J. Weberman, noted garbologist, Dylanologist: How come yippies live in luxury hotels with black maids?
A yippie: All hotels in Florida have black maids. What have you done for the anti-war movement, Weberman? You're just a garbage collector.
A. J. Weberman: Typical yippie élitism. What's wrong with garbage?
Voice in crowd: Yeah . . . recycle A. J. Weberman.

During this spat, which escalated in anguish and aggression as the afternoon wore on, I found myself standing on the sidelines clutching a tape recorder, hoping it symbolized my neutrality. Acquainted with identities on both sides, I was unable to endorse either team, yet again the victim of my own ambivalence. In a ritual act of self-recognition, I extended my hand for a portion of the birthday cake. The time had come to eat Jerry Rubin's words myself.

Since that day, things have gone from middle-aged to worse.

Ten years ago, as the first Sydney *Oz*es exploded on the scene, I was buttonholed: 'You'll change when you're middle-aged . . . everyone does.' I laughed and replied that Bertrand Russell had not succumbed. The turncoat syndrome is often interpreted as 'selling out', whereas its cause is more biological than economic. My fixation with generation gaps must have derived from the staggering decrepitude of those who ruled Australia when I was a teen. Despite its image as a land of thrusting bucks moulding the virgin landscape, the age of those in power was often over seventy.

Hence my knee-jerk inclination to draw a causal connection between the state of not being a teenager, and Stalinism. That's how youth culture swallowed me up.

Here I am in the next decade, having just completed thirty-one years before the mast and in a quandary about the future. I can't even join the squatters of Camden Town, knowing full well I'd be kicked out for making love to Begin the Beguine.

And *Oz* itself of late is read more from duty than pleasure. No longer symptomatic of a confident, inquiring consciousness, it regurgitates second-hand slogans and off-the-peg sleaze. It's a peacock posing as a gadfly, armed with a dildo and a Polaroid, pushing for some hair-brained utopia of copulation on the rush-hour tubes.

This is not a sign of a Great Leap Right. I have come to learn that those who hold opinions opposite to my own are not automatically disqualified from suffering deep and genuine concern for the human race. In their own way, I suppose, everyone does, with fuckall effect.

Since I arrived in England, in the wake of a guilty furore over the BBC's doco *Cathy Come Home*, the number of homeless families has doubled – despite welfare groups such as Shelter. As I write, Nixon is breaking new tonnage records with his Merry Christmas delivery of bombs to Hanoi. (In September, the number of orphans in North Vietnam topped a million.) A housewife who for years had been soothing bronchitis with regular cups of cannabis tea is gaoled for nine months, without a murmur from the media. The voices of radio newscasters are laden with fatigue as they begin their reports: 'Another five deaths today in Northern Ireland . . .'

People like me are prisoners of the past, haunted by statements uttered previously, mocked by the critics who leaf through old cuttings. Writing is hard labour because of the battle to express what I *really* feel and think as opposed to what I *ought* to feel and think. This struggle, however hypocritical it becomes at times, to be explicit, consistent and truthful, has rendered it impossible for me to sign on the dotted line of any particular brand of *ism*. This isolation breeds unhealthy interest in one's own psyche.

'. . . *if you have no personal history, no explanations are needed; nobody is angry or disillusioned with your acts. And above all no one pins you down with their thoughts* . . .'

(Don Juan to Carlos Castañeda)

Many survivors of the fast fading age of permissiveness seem to have retreated into themselves; only to discover a vacuum. So they set out on all sorts of highways and byways in search of today's Holy Grail. It is the era of the Big Search – a quest for the eternal high, through meditation, brown rice, alpha readings, guruism, primal screaming, Jesus freakery, LSD or a munchy, crunchy granola of them all. This yearning to find a meaning at least pre-supposes its existence, just as 'thirst is the surest proof of water'.

Carlos Castañeda offers a key chronicle of non-ordinary reality. Through the use of mescalin and peyote, as administered by a Yaqui Indian sorcerer, Don Juan, he is given a glimpse of what is labelled 'A Separate Reality', a fourth world, seductive in its morality and awesome in its potency. His adventures with Don Juan revive our interest in 'the magnificence of the world'. Magic is legitimized. Who can forget the scene of 'finding your spot', of cruising a given environment until you sense the place (seat, rock, log, or couch) which feels most 'at home', which imparts power? 'Like most intellectuals, my back was against the wall,' the elusive Castañeda told *Psychology Today*. 'I had no place to go . . . I thought all I could do was to make a mature adjustment to a life of boredom or to find ever more complex forms of entertainment, such as the use of psychedelics, pot and sexual adventures . . .' That is, until Don Juan, the man we all need to meet, arrives on the scene.

A young American doctor, Andrew Weil, recently published an account of how psychotropic drug-taking enlarged his attitude to healing. It is the gentle dialectic of a monk, confessing how insights gained when being high led to productive evolutions in his own character, improving the state of his mental health and finally promoting him to reject altogether the basic philosophical tenets of Western medicine, in which he was trained at Princeton. Since then, he has set off in search of the curative knowledge from the fast disappearing Don Juans of the Fourth World.

While I participated in the emergence of London's counter-community, both in private life and while working on *Oz*, I have always been handicapped by a copywriting mentality and an inability to remember much of what happened the day before yesterday. I tend to think of the Paris Commune as a mixture of the Moulin Rouge and a kibbutz. Yet up until the famous trial I felt marginally useful in propagandizing the Movement and denigrating the values of straight society, from which I always felt alienated.

Since then I have become adrift. It's a confusion born of privilege. Anyone stuck at the wrong end of a conveyor belt or sweating in a coal seam three miles under the North Sea should know who he's fighting and why. How pathetic to pick up the gauntlet of the State with a flourish of plagiarized slogans or to fight a journalist's revolution upon a barricade of underground press cards.

Somewhere, in the deep despairing luxury of my wallowing nostalgia, poised between *Boy's Own Annual* and a paperback Orwell, I sometimes pretend to lament the passing of crises as clear as the Spanish Civil War, when assistance from international volunteers was welcomed. Recruits were not dismissed as middle-class meddlers, but appreciated as dedicated idealists, who put Lee Enfields where their mouths were. It wasn't all napalm, personnel bombs and space age booby traps. You joined forces with a democratically elected government – if you'll forgive the phrase – affiliated with a wide spectrum of radical groupings. The enemy was ripening fascism, a filthy Church and the rehearsing war machines of Germany. To get there, you hopped on a train at Victoria station. They don't make wars like that any more.

Some of us accept the superstition that true artists have the power of self-fulfilment, that somehow their work is a battleground for resolving private, internal tensions. Life itself is an art form, and one object of the revolution is surely to give everyone access to their inner self.

I suppose in previous times those in this unsavoury mood, who were not fully harnessing their soul, would have whisked themselves off to rape a new frontier; gone West young man, mapped the Australian outback or set off in search of Dr Livingstone.

Even if ploughing through jungles could, these days, be morally reconcilable, there are not many left, and somehow driving a bulldozer ahead of the Brazilian highway isn't quite the same thing. And that last resort of the idle dreamer, the moon, has become, as the *Daily Express* noted with glee, the prerogative of 'squares, those who don't mind saying a prayer now and then, who look clean and are proud of their flag'.

Some people fill the vacuum by challenging the impossible, and winning. Not always for the glory and public acclaim – the like of which, say, Sir Francis Chichester could not have anticipated – but for its simple human self-enrichment.

The strange, deluded voyage of lone yachtsman Donald Crowhurst, as brilliantly reconstructed by two *Sunday Times* journalists, makes clear the allurement of global challenge and reveals the risks. Crowhurst was trapped in a myth of his own making, the sure-fire winner of the round-the-world yacht race, and when even modest success eluded him, he falsified reports of his progress. While drifting impotently around the Atlantic, he began to believe that Einstein was God and mathematics the key to the universe. Being neither unscrupulous nor heroic, yet fuelled by false hope, Crowhurst was left with the choice of ignominy or suicide. Malcolm Muggeridge has called this a saga of our time, and for once I agree with him.

Scratch a former member of the Youth-quake, and bleeds a little bit of Donald Crowhurst.

Sitting here mulling over who's going to pay my pension when I'm sixty-four, trying not to falsify my reports, searching for short cuts to Nirvana; still pondering how our energies can be fruitfully organized, but meanwhile, mostly like the unfortunate yachtsman, drifting man, just drifting.

'*If I should die, think only this of me*
That there's some corner of a foreign field
That is forever Woodstock.'

Oh, bullshit.

(*Oz 47*)

Postscript

Feckless, so feckless is how it seems to me now, looking back from my domestic life in the nineties, swinging through a range of joys and vexations each day. (Though I am happy to see that the 'hippie doctor', Andrew Weil, is now an eminent celebrant of the marriage between Western and alternative medicine, and that his latest book, *Spontaneous Healing*, is on the best seller lists.) Of course, I wasn't alone in my psychic disarray. 'The existential vacuum is a phenomenon that is both increasing and spreading', the psychiatrist Victor Frankl wrote at the time, citing statistics to show that the dog-days of activism, the end of the sit-ins and picketings, had sparked a flurry of admissions to psychiatric centres.

Soon after this piece was published, a letter lured me to Nimbin, a dying dairying town in Northern NSW, which had been chosen as the site of a bold experiment. 'Come and be part of the Aquarius Festival', one of the organizers wrote. 'Our object is to create a community more open, more joyous and more loving than the surrounding establishment society . . .' Why not? Two months before the festival, I reached this rural hamlet, set in a volcanic valley, whose 300 locals had agreed to host a student-funded gathering of tribes.

Waves of longhairs rolled off the bus, the facade of the moth-eaten café was being splashed with a psychedelic rainbow. In the alternative media office on main street (the only street), we crouched importantly on beer cartons and discussed the impending celebration. Aquarius would offer no set program, no superstars.

Festival-goers would be invited to stay behind after the lifestyle fair and become self-sufficient. 'It is wasteful to build the new', we agreed, 'when we can revive the existing.' This festival would trigger the recycling of Nimbin.

The mood was buoyant. Fingers pounded pre-war typewriters, giving birth to the *Nimbin Good Times*. 'Let's inject this whole region with energy and ideas,' urged a voice. 'Our festival will not be an end, but a beginning.'

It was to be an arts festival, yes, but not in the familiar sense of a slick marketing exercise, where culture is treated as a commodity and fed to docile consumers. Our most vital work of art, we agreed, was our lifestyle. The event only had one aim – to demonstrate an alternative way of being.

1
A Cheese Called Nimbin

*It was a family holiday in a town of the future, but
the past kept coming on strong. At the Saturday
market, my pre-teen daughter haggled over a silver
pendant – her first peace sign. My wife inspected
the tie-dye fashions and said, 'They're doing it
better than we did.' At the rock festival, the
biggest hit was a group in black leathers calling
themselves the Doors. 'Let's get outta here,' I
moaned, dragging my tribe off to the tour bus.
Little did I realize . . .*

1995:

Looking like the kind of tourist I once despised – shorts,
a silly hat, a camera; a wife and two daughters in tow –
I boarded the daily Backpacker Special at Byron Bay, an
upbeat coastal resort. Two young German women in torn black
leggings and T-shirts plonked themselves beside us, their
pierced lips pouting, defiantly amorous. Others from all over
Europe piled in; enticed to our mythic destination by tales on
the travellers' grapevine. We were bound for Nimbin.

The bus zig-zagged its way past beaches and lakes, scooping
up the young and the ragged from the budget hostels, which
have sprouted like gold top mushrooms. Noticeboards reeked of
mystery and camaraderie: *Campervan share-ride to Uluru, dig
for Opals at Lightning Ridge, abseiling for singles, scuba-diving
at night for beginners* ... At one lodge, tepees and igloos
dotted a winding stream, invoking images from Neverland,
with dreadlocked figures in feathers swaying on hammocks,

poring over maps. Byron's hinterland of green hills and mossy rainforest supports a thriving alternative culture, which so far has united to keep at bay the beast of multinational development.

The driver described how the countryside had been savaged by previous waves of Europeans – trees felled, rivers poisoned, weeds amok, fragile topsoil damaged by livestock. We nodded sadly. That was a time when Australia rode on the sheep's back. Now it's the backpack.

The gaudily painted Nimbin Special stopped for a sausage sizzle at Terania Creek rainforest, where the bush tucker tea was brewed from a native bush. Our driver and guide – a former stand-up comedian – impersonated 'straight' tour operators and spoofed folksy ballads on his guitar, adding a bizarre glee to the excursion. The girls from Berlin loosened up, revealing that rumours had reached them in Krakow of the place called Nimbin, where meditation was compulsory, everyone lived in communes and went shopping naked; each child had twenty mothers and marijuana grew from the roof of the police station. Dare I reveal to them that I was a formative player in this Nimbin Dreamtime?

After the famous Aquarius Festival, a ten day celebration of the counter-culture, a Woodstock Matilda, hundreds stayed behind to perpetuate the dream. They cleared the lantana, built communal farms, had babies, swapped lovers, harnessed power from the sun and the rivers, smoked dope, played the shakahachi flute by moonlight beside waterfalls, fought poverty and each other, danced, demonstrated, made masks and held more festivals . . . as decades of global yuppiedom passed them by.

The highlight of today's lunchstop was a 'nature walk' to Protesters Falls, named in honour of the massive green blockade from the Aquarius era, which rescued the rainforest. Our guide discoursed on 'bush tucker', passing around edible nuts and berries to the satisfying sound of feminist screams as we removed the leeches from up each other's shorts.

The bus paused on the crest of a hill. The quirky settlement below us would have been a ghost town by now, assured the driver, if it hadn't been for The Festival, the last stand of the counter-culture. It created such ripples that the town was reborn and a new national cheese was later launched in its honour. As it happened, I carried this cheese in my pack – Nimbin Natural, 'a great alternative', an emergency kid's-snack. Its label was a lyrical tribute to the achievement of the cheese's 'personality', the result of blending 'traditional Dutch, Swiss and English techniques', with a hearty input of 'health-giving acidophilus cultures, vegetarian enzymes', etc. Most importantly, it was 'allowed to mellow ... in environmentally controlled maturing rooms, during which time its unique AUSTRALIAN CHARACTER DEVELOPED'. Right on – mellow yellow – Nimbin's character in a nutshell.

The town's signpost incites a multicultural cheer from the back of the bus, as Jimi Hendrix screams through the speakers and the aroma of an ancient smoking herb billows through the air-conditioning. The Berliners kiss. The driver recounts historical tidbits from the days of The Festival, which had lured me home from my London basement. Here I had played the role of the flowerchild hotshot, swanning around in the nude, brow-beating students to set up a 1,000-acre commune – 200 dollars a share, I bought one myself – before flying off to New York to spend double that on a sportscoat at Bloomingdales. On our left, we are now passing that commune, Tuntable Falls, shimmering with geodesic domes, solar-powered sheds, riverstone cottages and galvanized iron yurts; the road not taken.

My daughter asks about the funny smell in the bus and what's that silly expression on Dad's face. 'He's having a flashback,' suggests The Missus, as my mind floods with memories of erections in the undergrowth ...

1973: Nimbin was waking at dawn with the sun, jumping into the chilly creek, bustling back to the campfire for a billy tea-and-toast breakfast and then deciding whether the rest of the day should be spent dawdling to the swimming hole, traipsing the crowded fields with the minstrels or moseying into town to collect organic veggies at the cost-price co-op (and sneaking off to the bakery for a meat pie). Acres of greenery sprouting with longhairs, all of them smiling. No awesome stage studded with superstars – this festival was us.

The site was a scene from an alternative Homes Exhibition. There were tepees, offering the magic of indoor fires and a touch of history, bamboo domes, grass huts, tree houses, parachute pavilions and, in our case, a humble, hired tent. With twilight came the fossicking for firewood among the felled gums, dragging the logs back to camp and setting off to replenish the water supply. Switching sensibly to woollen underwear, I groped irritably for the Lilo puncture kit and cursed the dotty stamina of the Hare Krishnas as they brayed till dawn, huddled in a circle on a hill, mocked by the giant gums standing dead against the bright escarpment.

I felt slightly the square outcast at this mass gathering. More hippies crammed in the outskirts of a one-pub town than were left in the rest of the world. You couldn't hear yourself think for the creaks of consciousnesses being raised. There were yogi men, gurus, Divine Lighters, space cadets, proselytizing Marxists, velvet-clad troubadours and a few Aborigines. Jesus was well represented, often in the form of Cliff Richard look-alikes, strumming up a storm near the war monument. Mostly, the doctrine of non-interference was paramount ('doing their thing, man'). One foaming-at-the-mouth Aquarian sat in the main road tilting at traffic until a town resident, a 'straight', bodily removed her from danger. Without the counter-culture, no matter how paradoxical and parasitical that concept may be, such people would be carted off in the greencart. But without the 'straight' she would have been run over by a truck.

You had to be alert to committing eco-atrocities, like soaping yourself in the creek or taking a car to the campsite. Each clan took its own rubbish to the depot, sorting it as: glass, metal, compost, or paper. After accidentally tossing an apple-core into the bin marked 'metal', I spent ten minutes feeling guilty, then rummaged within. That's how Nimbin got to you.

It's claimed that hippies are 'into ZPG', but not at Nimbin. Children grew on trees. Hundreds crowded the video monitors on logs to watch a new arrival, a live transmission of a baby being born among the gums, the doctor in T-shirt and jeans.

Shitting at Nimbin was public, communal and mixed . . . suntanning in unenclosed cheesecloth outhouses, where you made new acquaintances and exchanged gossip. The Christian contingent fought this demystification of the bowels by erecting their own privy of black PVC, guaranteed impenetrable by the human eye.

Crime was minimal. At UK rock festivals, kids stole each other's sleeping-bags and/or collapsed of hunger and horrible diseases. From Red Cross urns I'd ladled cocoa to shivering Glaswegians in beer-sodden clothes, with no money and nowhere to go. Conditions were so cramped and uncomfortable at the Isle of Wight that people slept knee-deep in the lavatories. Here there was little theft, no rapes reported, no violence.

As for drugs, where had all the Tambourine Men gone? I pricked my ears for all those plaintive calls – 'Acid, speed, grass, downers'. But no, all was quiet in the Nimbin night, with people huddled around their own campfires, smoking it less and enjoying it more. Perhaps, when people take Mother Nature as their dancing partner, the less they need drugs to provide a beat. Apart from the plainclothed plods from Sydney, stolidly trying to unload a rusty morphine kit, no one saw signs of the harder stuff.

Nimbin was an attempt at do-it-yourself decentralization. The official answer to overcrowded cities is – build more overcrowded cities. The student organizers of Aquarius wanted to tell city slickers that there's more to country living than *Flying Doctors*, and that playing a flute under a tree can be just as enthralling as paying to see the latest pre-packaged crap.

Nimbin was a thrilling manifestation of tribalism. We shared chores, we thought global, we tried to break the spell of Yankee rock. A tightrope-walker from France bedazzled the kids, the Bauls of Bengal blew us into a new dimension. We shared the odd beer with the locals, trying to allay their suspicions, and visited their rotted humpies, their starving dogs and realized what an easy road we had travelled. It was not a matter of going back to nature, as so many claimed, but of going forward with nature. Of living lightly on the land, learning about seasons, community, clowning and what the heck to do about plastic. Of seeing how many of us were still prepared to be counted, and learning how to live together outside an office. So many of us departed these fields with a new lease of optimism, with wild and romantic ideas. Nimbin lives, and the spirit of the Aquarius festival – the spirit of the blitz without the blitz – may one day take us by surprise.

Weeks later, converts were still buzzing around the north coast lecturing bewildered surfies on weed clearing, compost and organic farming. 'I'm off to the jungles up north,' announced an Aquarian in bellbottoms, 'to plant fruit trees.' Others will stay behind to start communes. The festival was truly regional, survival-oriented, healthy (hot dogs and hamburgers were hard to get, but I managed), anti-consumerist and high. Unstructured days in cattle country, navigating new human alliances, watching kids produce their own batiks, and chug-a-lugging Kick-a-Germ Joy Juice at the alternative health tent . . .

Most of us were nude some of the time, so studiously cool that tampons dangled like blind cords. Stray cops who wanted to 'mix it with hippie chicks in the showers' were identifiable by their beer guts. They never made it to the improvised saunas, down by the river, where the action was. A friend who entered an igloo of rusty galvo belching smoke reported that the traditional nudist taboo against having erections in public was now a thing of the past.

@)   @)   @)

Our bus comes to a halt; kids sit in the gutter rolling joints, tourists cram a string of cappuccino bars. On the shop-fronts of Nimbin, the psychedelic paint is peeling. Junkies loiter near the loo, bloodshot boozers lurch from the pub. It's a bad ad for recreational drug-use. Even so, the street is festive. There is laughter, children and dressing up; plus faint intimations of pride. From the rainbow region, activists have fanned across the world – to regenerate rainforests, to blockade warships, to seed the ideas of spirit and community. 'If you dream your dreams alone, they remain a dream,' proclaims a Nimbin settler, 'but the dreams you share become a reality.' The story of this town is testament to that, as is the potency of its myth. 'If Nimbin was in India,' says another, 'it would be declared a holy place.'

Our driver guides his gaggle of visitors across the road. 'Most of the original Aquarians have long disappeared,' he announces, as we file into the local museum. It is dark inside, crowded with the tattered memorabilia of my youth. A battered yellow Kombi van, fitted out with bongs, mattresses and Indian bedspreads . . . the way they used to be. A frisbee, a roach-clip, an embroidered Indian skirt, a faded copy of *The Politics of Ecstasy*, an Incredible String Band LP and a temple drum. Walls are plastered with stills, graffiti and shock-horror headlines of old – 'Nimbin tot has rabies'. Coins are scattered in a one-time recycling bin, funds for a park, a plaque or undetermined 'monument' to honour the first Aquarians. I recalled the mantra everyone sang here back then, which had irritated me with its sweetness: 'May the long time sun shine upon you, All love surround you, And the Pure Light within you, Guide you all the way home . . .' Back out into the brightness of the ratty flower-filled street. A teenager passes a fag to her friend and remarks: 'Last night's acid, wow. I had a flashback to the sixties . . . and I wasn't even born then. Incredible.' I, for once, am speechless, and the Berliners in black giggle, unaware of the ancient monument standing beside them.

(*The Observer/Nation Review*)

2
From Utopia to Bloomingdales

*In 1976 I flew to New York, chasing a woman I
loved, and was shocked by the scene. This was a
city I had associated with rebellion and vision,
ever since my first visit in 1968, when I hung out
with firebrand journos and watched the yippies
recount the results of their flower tests – to find the
best blooms to drop from a plane on a Central Park
love-in. Ancient history. Manhattan was gearing
up for the eighties, and I wasn't ready to bite the
bullet. Or was I?*

1976:

Who is this debonair creature staring in dismay from the
mirror in the menswear department? Surely not me, so urbane
in a silk-lined double-breasted woollen blazer with a $350
price tag, my first contemplation of a swish outfit since
starting off in Sydney's adland, all those years ago? Tailored
classics camouflage a scruffy frame – dashing, authoritative,
determined, that's how I look, almost handsome, on top of
the world, in charge of the future, going places . . .

Like all the rest, have I too come full circle? The hippie
leftover drearily reverting to class after a decade of denims
and defiance – me? – the soapbox radical, now marooned in
Manhattan with a dyslexic typewriter while old friends sip
Diet Pepsi and lecture me on the joys of stockbroking.

I teeter on the brink of materialism's giddy embrace, a colonial bumpkin at the altar of work-chic. 'It's not fashionable to
be poor any more,' sighs the tyro from *Rolling Stone*, cautiously

tapping out lines of white powder and inviting me places where jackets are mandatory. Numb to the turncoating of the élite, I am dismayed by the fevered apostasy of the rank and file.

A friend who once flew to Algiers in a camouflage outfit, to pay court to radical fugitive Eldridge Cleaver, is now a Wall Street textile broker, 'ripping off both buyer and seller', as she puts it. Eldridge found Christ, she capitalism. A former prankster, with whom I once ran from tear gas in Miami, is now a cut-throat literary agent. Already a millionaire, he is embarrassed by his former intimacy with celebrity rebels and cultivates a safer coterie. 'Julie and David are a wonderful couple,' he gushes, referring to the Eisenhowers. In a forest near Woodstock, I meet the bustling, charming landlord. 'How did you acquire so many cottages?' I ask. 'It all began when I was searching for places to hide out the Weathermen.'

Others, once legends of languor in the druggy backwaters of Ibiza and Marrakesh, are now stolidly behind profit and proud of it, remorselessly pounding themselves for past inertia and relieved to be back on the treadmill.

Hip merchandising is midwife to a litter of mini Rockefellers, stoked with coke and self-importance behind huge desks, fingering their concertinas of credit cards. With a stake in the system, having jumped from steerage to poop deck, they have no wish to rock the boat (no matter if it turns out to be the *Titanic*).

And why not? whispers an inner voice. Who wants to wring out the century in the Bowery, washing windscreens, forever the dutiful hippie enslaved to yesterday's slogans, aping the pauper deaths of *fin de siècle* decadents, mourned only by creditors?

While seeking to manoeuvre these thoughts into print, I meet a *Village Voice* editor who explains he once lived in a commune and hated it ('all our ideas came from books'). No longer an insecure freelancer, he's delighted to be . . . 'a boss now, it's so much more rewarding'.

Still numbed by the consistency of my first week's impressions, I click into Bob Dylan's *Rolling Thunder* TV special and watch it fizzle before my naïve eyes, as all involved radiate an inner ennui, with Joan Baez looking as self-satisfied as she had sounded in the *New York Times* a few days before: 'If I had the time, I'd fly to Paris for my clothes . . . I'm addicted to good things.'

And for the final cherry on the whipped cream (as if it's needed), the Manhattan autumn is ushered in with 'ethnic chic' – a gruesome parody of poverty in which Altman's department store crowns Oscar de la Renta 'king of the peasants'. Bonwit Teller announces: 'You've changed . . . we've changed. It begins with the new Julianelli boots . . . redefined in terms that are purely today . . . and, let's face it, far more at home in a Rolls than around a horse.'

You've changed . . . I've changed . . . but the world we all wanted to overthrow has not – if anything, its injustices are more entrenched, its inequalities more blatant than ever; only the cast of the ruling class has been shuffled around in order to conserve the myth of democracy.

Then, was it all in vain?

For many, the sixties was a surrogate World War Three. It struck not at Hitler, but at all the autocratic attitudes constraining our lives. Many were sacrificed and few are remembered. For each mythologized rock star drowned in a puddle of vomit, how many unknown flower children gave up the ghost?

Scores from the highly extended family of *Oz* magazine disappeared, if not to jails or asylums, then into permanent, sleazy oblivion. One secretary vanished down Harlem's smack alley, a distribution wizard conked out in a Moroccan cesspool, a black power protégé, Michael Abdul Malik, ended dangling from a gibbet in Trinidad . . .

Buddies turned out to be informers, communes crumbled, and hipness became a loaded .45. And was it worth it, after all?

It's a close decision; one crowded with ironies, millionaires, traitors and breakthroughs. Wars have ended, despots been dethroned, consumers made more muscular, closets abandoned, and genders blurred. For a generation, the achievement can be summed up with one observation: behavioural options have multiplied. The sixties let us take risks: to start a paper, to hit the road, to fight for a cause, to pick up a guitar, to play at politics, to go communal or merely to enjoy an extended vacation.

It's glib to assume that this eruption was the product of such definable issues as the draft, Vietnam, acid or subliminated parental rejection. Veils were wrenched from a deeper malaise. At the accepted experience of everyday life, people booed! Madness leapt briefly to the stage; humans actually gave away money, and love was a catchcry. This deeper dissent bubbled to the surface in May '68, with the breathless graffiti in Paris. 'Ten days of happiness already!'

But the spirit fizzled before the rocket ignited, and the projectile of revolutionary intent never struck its mark. Finally, the dropped-out lifestyle became vapid and boring, as it was bound to do, when based on the consumption of images unaccompanied by political thrust. Some can recall their turning points. 'When I finally made it to Kathmandu,' said an American friend, 'it was so squalid and revolting that I realized it was the end of the line.' He came home and joined a bank.

Only dullards set their teenage politics in aspic. Challenging one's convictions can take more courage than maintaining them, and it is stupid to be sour about all the sudden transformations: 'Be cruel to the past and those who would keep you there.' It's only entrepreneurs who want to reunite the Beatles, for the last thing we need is a replay of *Sergeant Pepper* or the Chicago Seven.

Those not in the spotlight are free to flipflop without ridicule. Personally, I shift from moods of progressive reconciliation with the system to weekends of hackneyed outrage. Now that the ethics have been tossed out with the Day-Glo, the tombstone can be formally inscribed: turn on, tune in, drop out, get a job, get *Rolling Stone*, get trapped.

Meanwhile, it's still corruption, poverty and dog-shit. More and more, life is mediated through images. The stranger at the bar who soaks up fifteen hours of television a day ('It's my hobby,' he said) is only doing explicitly what most of us do in a dream. Surrounded by phantoms, we are reduced to psychic passivity and copycatism. Drugs, psychiatry and lost weekends in the country do not dent the spectacle; they enhance it.

The faces on the subways and in the all-night supermarkets seem to sense what's in store for them; they emanate resigned hostility to life itself and ululate with powerlessness. Occasionally, a desperado dares to seek redress for an overcharged potato, but most of us tiptoe through the trolleys to the cash desk and make a pretence at following the flurry of figures. Why can't we control what's happening to us?

The sheer uselessness of most of the products is a metaphor for the sheer uselessness of the activity which conjured them up in the first place. Redundant consumption is the heartbeat of modern life, and billions flush fast through the machine to induce new fixations. Born free, we are everywhere in chain stores.

As oil was amphetamine to industrialism, so dope plays its part in moulding a market of consumer-junkies, many already isolated in fortresses of preposterous artefacts, shedding crocodile emotions over the latest media event.

In France not long ago, a college kid cut his own throat. He left behind a rambling, halting revelation of despair. His last words showed a spirit broken on the wheel of the educational inquisition. When the news spread, fellow students marched through town in solidarity. They held aloft placards that contained no words – just blank rectangles of white space.

Is not this sense of futility echoed elsewhere? Is it at the core of those spray-can cravings for identity on the subways?

Does it lie muffled behind the bashings of the elderly by the infantile? Is there a French connection to the rising tide of US student illiteracy? Blank placards, twisted thoughts . . . WE HAVE NOTHING TO SAY.

Perhaps the feet of the masses are quietly tapping to the tune of anarchy and yet no one is asking them to dance. As both pundits and politicians ache for the accoutrements of power, big bullies all, they cannot conceive a country of scattered self-contained communities and neighbourhoods, a polyglot cauldron of diverse alternatives defying rule from an apex.

Instead of always being about who goes to Washington, political discussion could centre upon why Washington goes on. Party politics are missionary-position politics and a healthy hunk of non-voters are signalling their receptivity to new ideas. And that doesn't mean Bolshevik nonsense.

The act of organizing a general takeover breeds a power more wildly rampant than the one overthrown and the bulldozers tend to mould a new gulag. (In 'liberated' Vietnam, Buddhists are burning themselves again.) Recognizing this, some wizened activists plug away at street level organizing without kow-towing to a fixed system, incorporating elements of Marxism, feminism and libertarianism. When the pressure is on, such slogging pays off, as shown in this letter from a London friend, where 40,000 trade unionists recently marched on parliament.

'The hospital cell I have been working in for three years is finally coming into its own. On the demonstration there was so much love about; clapping and cheering and embracing each new hospital delegation as it marched up . . . people so happy not to be working. Suddenly, there was a new depth. Here there is conflict, resistance, movement; we can fight together. Not that awful, finely honed individualism of the white American middle class who think you're mad if you're not as competitive as them, who make even relaxation an effort, who breeze about intimacy and friendship, which is all phoney and based on what your status is . . .'

Other friends have run off to the woods.

'Communes are thriving to a much greater degree than we had imagined,' report a couple who have published their findings as a book. 'The further away from regular families and cities and careers that we get,' they write, 'the less obnoxious and self-centred the kids get. Which says something about the regular American family and is the challenge of commune life to us.'

Times have changed but the choice remains: collaborate or resist. Maybe it's two steps forward and one step sideways – taking care of survival, but pushing out the boundaries. If you can't sink the state, save the whale. Who wants to be short-haired on the inside too?

(*SoHo News*)

3
Dancing on the Rock

A boulder sparks a sob . . .
a nondescript hill a scream.

*The sports jacket did the trick. In 1977 I accepted an assignment from a publisher to fly to Delhi and interview the incarcerated 'hippie killer' Charles Sobhraj, about whom I later wrote a book with Julie Clarke, the journalist I had followed to New York. It took two years. (*Time Out *crowed: The Copywriter for Utopia gets an Honest Job.) Julie and I returned to Australia to see our families and launch the book, and decided to settle in the Blue Mountains west of Sydney. A daytime talk show hired me as a 'social commentator', and I contributed to a variety of publications – this one for the London* Observer *in 1986, on the Green Dreamtime.*

1986:

I held another in my arms, running my hand up a smooth, silvery limb, and lost myself in the brisk summer scent. This beauty I had long admired; a Scribbly Gum tree, whose trunk and limbs are strangely anthropomorphic and covered in scribbles left by grubs in the bark. (In kid's lore, these are the bushland's newspapers.) My odd embrace says something about the state of social relations in Australia – some communicate more deeply to trees than each other.

Even city-dwellers are being forced to come to terms with

how they feel about their forests and flora, a sign of an emerging debate, which cuts across ages and styles. It's not just a matter of 'liking trees'. To save a rainforest, would you bury yourself up to the neck in a muddy hole, chained to a root, in front of the growling bulldozers? In North Queensland many young people did, despite the determination of the dozer-drivers.

William Wordsworth, the Priest of Nature, espoused the need to rejuvenate the soul in the great outdoors. It is the ease with which this right is exercised here which makes Australia . . . Australia.

Don't come for the dinner parties. Don't come here stalking jazz cellars for Rimbaud or you'll end up like all the rest, in the sticks with Rambo. Expatriate hot-shots often complain to the foreign media how they were savaged – on their last sprint home – by the great spirit dingo of boredom. It lunged at them from every corner, between the airport and their suite at the Regent Hotel.

They miss the whole secret of living here; which has nothing to do with inner-city chit-chat. Australia is one of the few countries in the world where it is still possible to get away from other Australians. Being thrashed about in the surf, impenetrable to conversation, is heaven enough. You can disappear into ravines, raft the rivers, abseil the cliffs – all for free. Visitors miss this rapport which locals have with the land.

Forget the manicured fields and planted groves. I remember dragging one cosmopolitan traveller up the little hill near my mountain home. Looking across the endless spread of gums and banksias, shimmering blue in an oily haze, and the cliffs dropping into fern-filled canyons, he remarked, 'Isn't it depressing?' Not to me, but he must have been moved by a sense of irrelevance. No evidence of human presence marred the ancient-terracotta cliffs; not a single tree or shrub was planted by human hand; the land itself, a national park, was not owned by any one person. All this is thrilling, after the cultivated landscapes of Europe, where generations have trod . . . have trod. The valley beneath my window boasts no architectural lineage of civilization, and Socrates never strolled the escarpment inventing hypotheticals. But that doesn't mean the bush is without its intimations of wisdom.

This love of land is more than therapy, a new aesthetic or our response to the rising costs of flight. It is also reparation for its maiming by the First Settlers. The felling of millions of acres of trees was more to do with neurosis born of nostalgia than good farming. Old-timers still scratch their heads at the rising salt and degraded soils, while merrily ring-barking the eucalypts.

Other Australians are making a stand. The computer programmer who downs tools and moves to the bush, spending all spare time restoring the diversity, while funding the project by being a potter. Or the rainforest couples north of Cairns in handmade pole houses, studying one of the finest collections of primitive flowering plants in the world; every second one an 'undescribed species', and now, because of an unnecessary road, 'green dinosaurs'. Seven unique species of marsupials under threat, including two kangaroos . . . The most creative of my friends, painters, craftspeople, fashion designers, cull their muse from the indigenous kingdom.

Yet compared to the aborigines, our love of the land is raw and awkward. An isolated aboriginal settlement in Western Australia acquired a video unit. When a tribesman played his tape of scenery to the community – long slow pans of sloping rock and stunted trees; nothing striking – viewers wept with emotion. A boulder sparked a sob; a nondescript hill a scream. (Some had never set foot in the area, recognizing it from songlines.)

Another aboriginal encampment which I visited had relocated itself hundreds of miles away from whites, to the 'red centre'. (An area of over half a million square miles, it is, after the polar caps, the most sparsely settled patch of land on earth.)

The founders were bent on reviving tribal culture. An aboriginal woman of high degree was trying to wean children from sniffing petrol with legends and dance and lessons in scrounging bush tucker. Most of the initiated men were away for the weekend – watching soccer. (The kids too were probably yearning for hot dogs and video games.) Camped by the river was a Marxist Theatre Company from Melbourne. Wild-eyed and dusty, they talked of 'collecting images' and 'workshopping' amidst the spinifex. With a government grant, they were filming a documentary of their experience. From nowhere, a mini-bus pulled up, disgorging a troupe of young Christian campers from foreign countries – Japan, Mexico, Germany – who began to regale the tiny tribe with a hymn painstakingly sung in the local Pitjantjatjara language. Yet another vehicle lumbered to the dry river bed. Three dusty naturalists emerged with skins of extinct animals, wanting to know their dialect names. To this bedlam must be added my own film crew – manifesting more boom-mikes than boomerangs. At least we came not to loot but to learn. It is on such strange desert nights at a campfire, under brighter stars, with dingoes howling on the distant hills, that one senses the growing reassessment of what it means to be Australian.

There was yet another, more permanent group of whites at the settlement. A couple with three children under the age of five, who were there as low-paid advisers to the aboriginals. They had happily left their parents' prosperous lifestyle for a tin hut with last-leg appliances, hundreds of miles from the nearest shop. They loved it. Their glow was more than a desert tan. This network of non-consumers who are infiltrating the outback and fusing tribal lore, radical ecology and personal dedication may never get to see the Louvre.

For the majority, Australia's virtue is still its material abundance. Despite high youth unemployment, there is a feeling that the true go-getter, the exuberant door knocker, can make a quid. A brawny local delivers my order of ready-mixed cement. As I huff and puff with the wheelbarrow, he tells me how he plans to retire at thirty-five – a story I've heard many times before in this country and actually seen come true. Still in his twenties, he had struck a good deal on a second-hand truck, which he was now 'owner-driving' for a fat fee, and he had applied for a McDonalds franchise. This man had no special advantage; just boundless optimism and self-confidence, bred of egalitarianism. A change from the rage and despair of urban rioters. While his values are not mine, it's cheerful to live in a land where the dice aren't always loaded against the punters.

On a recent trip to Greece, I met young tourists from all over Europe who seemed to dread going back to their homeland. 'Too competitive . . . too cold . . . too serious . . . too conformist,' they complained. At their age, I must have dreaded going back to mine – still, their sense of alienation is opposite to the puppy pride of today's young Australians, who call their country . . . Oz.

For us baby-boom former expatriates, Oz has come to mean a source of strength and regeneration, despite all the hideous philistine crap. In the old days, from the little tyrannies of suburban minds, there was no escape. Not like London, where you could always cure those basement blues with a weekend in Paris. But being here now, I've found its equivalent – the direct flight to Uluru (formerly Ayers Rock).

The Rock has become a mystical magnet for Australians and foreign visitors alike; a wonder of the world. Walk in a Dreamtime daze around its five and a half miles of prehistoric, painted caves and sacred springs. Most tourists treat the Rock as a drive-in movie, parking at the official sunset viewing area and gasping with each changing hue. Twenty miles to the west of the Rock lie the Olgas, or Katajuta, a clump of giant domes which are, in the words of their European discoverer, Ernest Giles, 'the more wonderful and grotesque'. It is like some ruined, ancient city on another planet; the domes glowing red hot on the sands; with its eerie Valley of the Winds and

stunning gorges; so unexpected and perplexing in the middle
of a desert.

It is because the creation of these landmarks had nothing
to do with humans that they impact so powerfully on our
psyches. The symbols counterpoint the country's materialism
and their potency betokens a higher force than the capital,
Canberra . . . or Culture. You come away altered, enriched with
a measure of indigenous veneration. Europe can draw deep into
its past for spiritual refreshment; our own flashbacks reek of
rum, floggings, sodomy, massacres, scurvy and despair. For
generations, Australians have fled to Europe for nourishment –
perhaps only noticing the extent of our desert from a Boeing's
window – whereas now that Uluru is our national symbol, locals
are learning to contemplate their own country's monolithic
navel; protruding, chameleon and sacred.

'The Rock is a supernatural energy source', according to some
of the keener new-agers, 'a beacon which lets other intelligences
know there is life on Earth'. Its 'mysterious force' has been
likened to the Bermuda Triangle and some 'attuned' visitors
report losing all sense of time. The Pitjantjatjara believe that
during Creation it changed from a low sandhill to its present
form, 'miraculously'.

And so we plod home to the city with shiny eyes . . . perhaps
to a dinner for an expatriate just landed, warming up for the
TV tour. 'Don't tell Clive how much Michael Parkinson is
paying me,' shrills the famous voice above the champagne and
silverware, 'he'll be furious' . . . News from the glowing capitals,
a lifetime away from my moody mountain eyrie, didn't I 'miss
the gossip'?

The centre . . . the bush . . . the sea . . . it all sounds so corny
across the sorbet. 'So much recreation will kill your mind,'
scolds an expatriate mate, who believes that to struggle and
to suffer is the key to wisdom. Isn't there already a surfeit
of sadness and cynicism? ('The learned doubt, the chatter of
cultured apes / which is called Civilization over there' – A.D.

Hope.) Here, it's great to be alive, great to make a difference, to work with others, shaking off the spell of our progenitors, making something new out of something so very old.

Thirty years ago, Bill Haley and the Comets exploded on to this colonial scene, disrupting the staid rituals of conformity and inner death. We broke loose, and thousands of young Australians rocked around the world. Now Halley's Comet is due for a comeback, the real thing this time, seventy-six years since its last sighting, and here we are, ensconced in our mountains, beaches and deserts for a view of the lightshow. Still a little loony, still dancing; but this time the music's our own.

(*Observer*)

Wrestling 4 the Weed

*'I've looked into the face of marijuana ... and
lived to tell the tale.' (Leonard Cohen live on* The
Mike Walsh Show)

*Public discussion is rare on the highs and lows
of getting high, considering the widespread use
of pot. Every so often, I blew a joint, sat at the
keyboard and tried to unravel my thoughts – at
least until my head crashed on to the space-bar.*

1975:

It has been proposed that cannabis users be subjected to periodic
intelligence tests, and that the Education Department digs out
our High School results for comparison. To what purpose?
Dopers are willing to trade a few IQ points for an expansion of
consciousness, realizing that the more they inhale, the less they
excel at playing grown-ups. Cannabis loosens us up, encourages
candour of intercourse and pops bright ideas into our head. Of
course, if the user is already a shit, then dope merely makes him
more of a shit.

And it can create dependence. Don't your friends become
tense, morose and lustless without the weed? That's why most
of them will reach for any old plastic bag of oregano, mint
and animal tranquillizer, so long as they're charged $30 and
told it's fresh from Sumatra.

Dope is both a product of decadence and a tool to transcend
it – depending on whose finger's on the joint.

Too many heads parallel the frailties of capitalism with an

intemperate, howling, suckle-me-daily desperation, a more =
better consumption ethic. Marijuana is too important to be
another Coca-Cola. Rather, it is a precious liqueur, to be passed
around moonlit terraces when you're in love with the rhythms
of life and want to dance with your brain cells. (The beat of the
city can make us run away from the stone, boring an escape
hole of rock music, instead of running along *with* it.)

Dope stretches acceptance of new ideas and showers you with
insights, some of which still make sense in the morning. While
it can enhance creativity, one's formative highs are generally
on the lowly wavelength of 'fanciful hedonism'. That sensual,
receptive, lazy, indulgent, watching-bad-tv, munchy-munchy
state of suburban bliss. Junk glitters. Peeling wallpaper dazzles
the eyes and its patterns reek with hidden significance, a
passing phase.

Dope is self-medication for depression: for those occasional
afternoons of internal rainfall, when the world dims and you're
looking across a wintry St Kilda beach (grateful for the head
cold that blocks the smell of the seaweed), surveying the sludge
and the seagulls among the Orchy bottles, hemmed in by a blur
of roaring cars on one side and, on the other, by tankers drifting
into port . . . Oh, yes, then can a whiff of Queensland heads
rob the occasion of its awesome grunge, converting a leaden
twilight into a silvery, meditative buzz. But to use the drug
solely for bolstering such a mood is to be a slave to it. Rather
than deck out mediocrity with tinsel, save it for more creative
adventures; the well trodden gateways being music and sex.

The first mindblast turned millions of ears into headphones,
and I can't believe everyone wasted so much time. Wasted? I
suppose if it hadn't happened, most of us would still be tuned
into the Top 40. The humble herb is still the denim of the drug
culture, coming back year after year to percolate through to
the denizens of the outer suburbs.

Sexually, grass makes you take risks, and in the kitchen it
leads you to throw away the cookbook and conjure up your

own culinary delights . . . or horrors. 'Liberty,' said Mill, 'is doing what one desires,' and getting stoned dredges those desires from the depths, freeing them from layers of habit and repression.

Qualifications:

1. Cannabis is definitely a drug dangerous to some personalities. Crazies become crazier. That pixilated nerd who 'always wanted to try it' can turn into a maniac with visions, a psychopath receiving transmissions from Mars through the speaker embedded in his brain, now coming towards you with the breadknife . . .

2. Memory is vulnerable. One friend watched his brother walk into a room and realized he'd forgotten his name (he quit). The effects of excess include idleness, amotivation, zombieism – educated smokers end up rationing their intake.

3. Heavy smokers are often light achievers. The weed gnaws away at self-discipline and can turn life into a muddle . . . Just like it has in Morocco, where kiff is the national pastime and has reduced, one suspects, a proud culture to a bloodshot shambles.

4. There's no such thing as an entirely safe drug, so why expect cannabis to be an exception? Stay on top of it, use moderately. I once ran a grass joint through a tar-testing machine (as issued by the anti-cancer council) and the result was horrifying. At first suck, the filter paper oozed with sludge. Be warned.

5. The merchandising of the dope culture is hazardous to social health and this chronicling of creative flashpoints does not constitute endorsement of the scene as a whole.

Isn't this depressing? And I haven't even mentioned the dangers of driving stoned or its impact on fertility (intending parents should take a long break).

Crucial to a final verdict is the long-term effect on character; which in the end is what you're stuck with. Here again, one must distinguish the foggy addict who cloaks self-hate in a cannabis cloud from the abstemious pragmatist – the one who uses with reverent caution, never for a moment forgetting the power of the drug. The trick is to swing between two states of consciousness – not reside permanently on either shore. Therein lies boredom, or madness.

TO CONTINUE, cannabis can be a social drug and one of solitude. Its impact is tribalizing. If it hadn't been for dope, I wonder whether those soft-bellied, middle-class, draft-dodging kids of the American sixties would have run the gauntlet of Chicago billy clubs to the guns of Kent State, so changing history. They sensed the mischief of Watergate, long before Woodward and Bernstein sculptured the plot.

Cannabis is a wonderful drug to read by. Some it speeds up; myself it slows down, intensifying and isolating special phrases and thoughts, allowing me to linger over outcrops of elegance, instead of it all blowing by, like so many snowflakes. Reading is my music. And writing. A portion of genuine Buddha stick has me belting away at the keys as though on a soul-organ, with the head a festival of ideas, pounding, pounding, with the wind in the hair, and fire in the fingers . . . until catatonia sets in. On re-examination next morning, you sometimes wish you'd spent the night more usefully, say watching the *Best of Homicide*, but not always . . . and after many months, one learns to match wavelength with weed. (Norman Mailer said he tried dope for a while, then gave it up, which in view of his later writings is hardly an advertisement for abstinence.) Champions in many fields of human endeavour, including surfing, painting, football and glass-blowing, have admitted to me how dope helps them do it.

One of the disadvantages of this speedy age is that people have sacrificed the need to think for themselves. I like marijuana because it stops one shoplifting from the supermarket of contemporary ideas . . . inducing the desire to grow your own.

The mystic fad is not unrelated to cannabis use. Austere

modern cultists often begin with the remark: 'I used to smoke ten joints a day, with acid at the weekends . . .' Soul-searching is a spin-off from reefer madness (Oh, well, it's better than scratching out Lotto). Everybody reaches a plateau, a victim of the law of diminishing returns. At such times it's best to sit it out straight for a while and observe the differences.

Dope is prone to make men cry – *not* in the morose self-abasing wash of alcohol (with which it doesn't mix at all) but in a humanizing adjustment to the agonies of going deeper, of putting life before policies. This burst of spontaneity can lead to a more adventurous embrace of romantic ideas about how society could be transformed.

I suppose this is the syndrome of . . . anarchist drift, which, however inadequate, is at least some sort of response to the world which rages outside the head: of terror, torture, hunger and decay. Each day we are bombed out with more information and less meaning. (Future shock is media overkill.)

There is urgent demand for new ideas, and quicker triggers of consciousness, some of which will emanate from a stoned haze.

Hunter Thompson once said that without drugs he would have ended up with the mind of a third-rate accountant. Doctors have described how they used the high to overcome phobias. Friends of mine who've smoked for decades, especially women, credit grass with balancing out their warring selves. These veterans – of course I'm biased – are more compassionate and complicated than the ambitious dried prunes who foreswore any inner experimentation and stayed straight, always working back at the office.

Sometimes when I meet old people who've led narrow and cautious lives, fussing over their instant coffee, I wonder why they seem so incurious about things, why their conversation is a series of trite repetitions. It is as though a whole dimension of joy and wonder has been denied them.

Harnessing a high does not have to be like a slug of Scotch.

It can be used to sharpen worthy instincts, shape honourable aspirations; even to entice you into realms previously decried. One moves on from squandering good grass on bad movies or dull company. For many, drugs have opened doors to new techniques, from which, looking back, one closes the door on drugs. This wild plant has started plenty of spiritual treasure hunts. To wallow, to consume, to depend . . . is to drown. Its basic ethic is the opposite to that of the society in which we live – that is its great secret – less is more – and none at all . . . is maybe, in the end, what all of us are aiming for.

(*Nation Review*)

Postscript

'Clang! Honk! Tweet! OOOoooOOOoooOOO! EEEEeeee-EEEE! Zow! Pow! Sproing! Zont! Flash! . . . Pretty good stuff we have here, brother!'

The Fabulous Freak Brothers

5
From Playpower to Playpen

Two views on child-rearing, ten years apart.

Who would have thought it would ever happen to me? Parenthood. I made as much fuss as possible, of course, virtually delivering the baby live on national television. Proud father in crumpled pyjamas, public lectures on the drawbacks of disposable nappies, hot tips on breast feeding . . . and so on, until the novelty wore off – about the next day. Trouble is, there's no escape. Such an outrage, the ordeal of fatherhood, and as soon as I got a good night's sleep – a few years down the track – I bared my soul to the world.

1985:

We three men sat in this ramshackle house by the ocean, savouring the rhythm of the pounding waves and waiting for the next tantrum. In the next bedroom, raw egoes were simmering. A gust of wind crashed a door. I glanced at the man opposite, moodily tapping his fingers on his knee, and wondered whether Ricky also felt strange about being here, on-edge and apprehensive.

It was a scene from *Key Largo* – except we weren't mobsters. Our wives were shut in the video room, editing tape. On this sweltering Saturday afternoon the fathers had agreed to mind the children. And when my daughter staggered from the bedroom holding a fluffy giraffe, her nappy fell off. Ricky's mouth twisted into a sneer: 'Still stumped by disposables?' he asked and both men laughed. Their kids were older than mine. Then they grilled me on toilet training. It was a movie all right – three edgy men on a windswept coast and I was playing the wimp. This was . . . *Crèche Largo*.

How did I get here? What process had led a selfish swashbuckler – had led us all – to abandon the afternoon's other attractions? It was connected with feminism, of course. The three women zapping the video bank were no doormats, but it was much more than that. We were here because of a changing concept of fatherhood.

From the outside it can seem absurd, pathetic. That drooling beefcake at the beach with a garden spade labouring over sandcastles for his indifferent toddler. The dowdy dad on the fringe of the party stooped under the weight of a baby in a backpack – his wife kicking up her heels with a bigshot. Our clothes hideously stained. Our eyes, which hang low in the sockets, tinged with the envy of herding too many old-time adventurers on to the Marrakesh Express. Not going, but waving.

There's an occasional jaunt to the in-laws in a car encumbered by highchairs or the thrill of hiding the Minties at the treasure hunt; movies unseen, books unread. Gone are the delights of those faraway childless years . . . And yet, when some men become parents, they hardly miss a beat.

'I didn't see my first son, Julian, grow up . . . I was not there for his childhood at all. I was on tour . . .' So said John Lennon, whose own father had been similarly absent. In emotional terms, this 'absence' applied to my father and many of his contemporaries.

Around four, I was encouraged to hide in the wardrobe as a jokey welcome to a uniformed stranger – my father. Fresh from the war, he remained through the years affable and remote; lost at the office, the pub, the tennis club. Sometimes we strolled down the hill together for a swim at Balmoral Beach, but soon it was time for me to go back to boarding school. That's the way it was – such a waste.

Had I become a father at an earlier age, before the gender upheaval, I probably would have repeated the pattern.

Instead, on my first nervous night at the inner city birthclass I was told to lie on my back on the floor. 'Imagine there is a pool of water in your stomach and a baby floats in it,' said the voice, 'and soon you will be pushing this baby through an underground river and out into the ocean . . .' she intoned, launching the class into deep meditation and the men into unusual convulsions. As the weeks went on, strapping yobs groaned, pushed, practised their Kegels, panted and dealt with pain. Comparing all this, up to the birth of our baby at home, to my own father's potshotting of Japanese in New Guinea at an equivalent time in his life, gives one clue to the discrepancy in parenting styles. Another is fashion.

By the time Lucy was a kicking and screaming vortex of responsibilities, I had already become familiar with the New Father. He looked haunted and forlorn, his face betraying a secret ache for two weeks' big game fishing with the boys? No, mostly, as he flopped about in the chaos of his Romper Room house, the New Father radiated a soppy joy. I remember a New Year's Day when various rakes and globetrotting bachelors hired a boat for a picnic on a deserted beach. Only one was a father, a New Father, who took his toddler in the water and threw him into the air, caught him and then threw him higher still . . . higher and higher the little boy went and louder and louder was his laughter. The gossiping stopped and all the rakes rushed into the water to share in the joy of the game, drawn by the high between parent and child; a high strange and unbounded.

The essence of New Fathering is being there. It is nurturing the luminous curiosity of childhood, not stifling, misleading or fleeing it. Yes darling, of course we can melt the jelly crystals, but not on top of the keyboard.

Being a New Father is bad for business – upwardly mobile he is not. In immortal verses, the metaphysical poets dealt with the problems of combining the spiritual life with worldly affairs. Who deals today with the balance between ambition and immersion parenting? Feminists lamented the career costs of child-rearing, then organized crèches so they could rule the world. For generations, men have valued ambition above commitments to infants. Now, as they cumbersomely readjust their priorities, they suffer bouts of resentment against the mothers – off again to the office, to yoga, aerobics or Depilation Row. Like Marianne Faithfull, I lament the lack of trips through Paris in a sports car.

Brilliant careers take time ... and time, suddenly, is disappearing.

After questioning our obsession with Reaching the Top ('exciting, not satisfying'), one author, David Stewart (an academic father of five), points out that 'it is a rare personal accomplishment to be so significant as to make any great difference fifty years later, but the way you raise your children will make a difference fifty, even a hundred years hence ... Generation after generation benefits.' This view is not endorsed in our society, which seems to be run by people estranged from their offspring. Why?

Who dares comment, when none are immune from a similar destiny? In the parenting game there are no guarantees and many a syrupy mum and dad have driven their children to the other end of the world. Heroin, however, is an extreme rejection. That so many bright youngsters are choosing slow suicide can't all be blamed on the bomb ... or the pusher. It might say something about bonding, the lack of ... or 'absence' or a love too silently expressed. The tale of a father driven to seek the highest office in our land has recently been publicized with his tears on television for an addicted daughter. Were these too few and too late – who knows? The scene became a metaphor. Other figures of authority were shown to have fathered junkies ... and we all felt uneasy at the publicity. Are such tragedies really 'inexplicable' and 'private' or do they, beyond the headlines, have implications for us all?

I know a man, now retired, with a close-knit, loving family. When young, he had an exotic profession which whirled him around the world. As soon as his first child was born he resigned and took a duller job on lower pay. He wanted to spend the weekends building billycarts and doll's houses. I used to sneer. Now I realize how heroic it was; sacrificing all to just . . . being there.

New Fathering has its dangers; of which the first is Over Indulgence. In the rush to compensate for the coolness of their own parents, the new dads stretch tolerance to the point of insanity. If not their own, their friends'. It is one thing to take toddlers to dine with grown-ups, even to sit them at the same table. But when the screaming fits begin and the chop bones fly, the besotted dad beamingly filches missiles for his child from guests' plates and remains oblivious to the appalled glances and stilted conversation. It's just another time bomb, this toddler tyrant at the table.

Another danger is . . . Cracking Up. All single parents – to whom I offer a heartfelt salute – will know what is meant. Couples who work to erratic deadlines find it hard to get help and men of a certain age are used to prolonged bouts of serene concentration. Alas, no more. When the pressure builds up I dream of the Foreign Legion. 'Just nicking out for some Gauloises,' I shout, striding towards the travel agent.

And friends change. Staying with bachelors, gay or otherwise, is fraught with catastrophe. After a few hours, grim-visaged hosts trail you with a dustpan and brush. Their prissy abodes, shrines to order and modernity, are no match for anarchy. I used to be the same. Mothers of teenagers now delight in reminding me how ghastly I was when they once visited my basement with a toddler – 'Shit, your brat spilt jelly on *Astral*

Weeks.' How reassuring, these days, to be guest in homes that are already junkyards.

Other values are changing, almost imperceptibly, and I'm too nervous to examine the process: attitudes to abortion, in-laws, dinner parties, spiders, spring, music, Manhattan . . . And when a child gets sick, the whole world shrinks to the size of a diving bell. Mentioning this to a young father, he replied: 'That's good, isn't it?'

'What do you mean?'

'That you felt such pain.'

I suppose it is. There are some things which don't come in books. People think that New Fathering is solely at the behest of the child (as an old friend said of me: 'he's trapped, trapped in a web of love'), but what gets you through the night is the certainty of inner enrichment.

In a letter to a newspaper, a couple explained why they sought an abortion: 'We felt unequal to the demanding task of properly raising a child . . . More importantly, we were unwilling to inflict the war-obsessed society in which we live on any child of ours.' Surely everyone feels unequal to the task of raising a child, none more so than the fumbling fathers of today, belatedly breeding. If we all stopped because of Bomb Culture, then the holocaust might as well have already begun. It is a new breed; lovingly nurtured, emotionally sound and spiritually evolved, that is our best ally, as impossible are the odds. Isn't it worth a try?

(Matilda)

Postscript

One expert claims that competent parenting of a child yields one million dollars in benefits to society, while every incompetently raised child costs society two million dollars in crime, welfare payments and other burdens.

Flashback 1973:

I Want Some Too, Grizzle Grizzle . . .

*As ashamed as I am of this outburst, it is included
as evidence of the ignorance and self-obsession that
can consume a roaming and childless commentator
on the human condition.*

For anyone alive and not depressed by ritualistic domesticity,
nothing is more oppressive than to be visited by an old
friend with new child. For all their pretty curly locks and
corduroy romper suits, today's young kid is a nasty, slimy,
titty-tattling, sugar-addicted, soiled bundle of rapacious ego
and untrammelled greed. My first law of kidology is that it is
impossible to have an intelligent conversation with an adult
human in the presence of its offspring.

One must conceal one's distaste, turning a blind eye to the
spilt ice cream and a deaf ear to the ceaseless interruptions.
Any hint of impatience is greeted with defiance and even the
most broad-minded parent is resentful of any reaction to their
progeny except flattery.

In more civilized climes children look after each other. They
disappear in groups early in the morning and are responsible
for each other in the logical pecking order of age group,
making them aware of their place in the scheme of society.
They are open, loving and loved. In some Asian communities,
parents *never* hit a child and corporal punishment at school is
unknown.

But in Australia, ugh. One can't have a quiet conversation
with mum, 'cause the kids are glued to *Sesame Street*'. If one
sneaks to the kitchen, then it's: 'Mummy I want some too,
grizzle grizzle.' With more than one child, it's a household

row every minute. 'It's mine, no mine, no mine . . . Gimme, gimme, gimme.'

The more kids in a home, the lower the IQ. Of course, the pressure to procreate is often irresistible. Much of this 'fruit of my loins' stuff still abounds, plus a fear of a lonely old age. And despite their revamped image, some women still use the concept of kids like a lump of cement – to keep their partnership together. Love or propinquity apparently isn't enough; let's do something efficient and symbolic, let's reproduce. All this before they've hit thirty.

Have you noticed how the mental development of parents begins to sag once the Farex, nappies and those unsavoury cans of Heinz babypap overflow into their life? (Making homosexual households a breath of fresh air.)

You owe it to kids, once you're stuck with them, to equip them properly, with good instincts and bright ideas; which must be exhausting. So wait around awhile – the earth is quite replenished enough, and the interesting challenge of the future is not merely to survive, to raise a dreary little family, but to flip out first on a few dimensions, acquire some soul, kindle your own spirit.

Cheerful human beings who enjoy life and are creative stem from societies *not* centred around the tight parent/child insulated relationship of the modern family, no matter how hip.

The uncanny unpleasantness of today's kids has a cosmic purpose – nature's own contraceptive; an absolute antidote to the reproductive instinct. For tailing off the human race it's sure better than free transistors; nature has created a situation of voluntary withdrawal from reproduction. The thinking, sensitive classes are abandoning the whole horrible myth of parenthood, and none too soon.

(*The Living Daylights*)

6
Opium, Gin-Slinging and Deep Ecology

One of the highlights of my time on a national talkshow was taking a film crew to India and shooting from the hip. The aim was to be spontaneous, off-beat, and to accentuate the positive . . . against all the odds.

1984:

At two in the morning the scene at Bombay airport was grim. The arrival lounge was carpeted with litter, and stank. The mood of our co-travellers – rarely happy-go-lucky in flight – had sunk to surly despair. Like *habitués* of Death Row, they lugged their huge Sony TV sets and video recorders towards the customs gauntlet. A rotund Sikh threw up, confirming my doubts about the airline's Beef Wellington.

Once through the snail-paced formalities, we faced another queue. This one for a ticket to catch a taxi. A line of identical black Ambassadors stretched from the kerb to the horizon – a home away from home for the drivers, who reportedly waited fifteen hours for a seven dollar fare and slept in their cabs. Or didn't sleep. Ours seemed to be finally nodding off as he nuzzled speeding trucks laden with bricks. My wife gripped the back of the driver's seat, while I stared at the string of slums, as sad and silent as a cemetery in the pre-dawn hours. A friend who had spent too long in India once remarked: 'All the talk of karma . . . just to be born in India is bad karma.'

It took only minutes for Bombay to break my determination to 'go with the flow', which, in this taxi, was too fast. Stupidly, I had quelled the urge to remonstrate – who wants to tell a local how to drive? Too late. Our cab zoomed into the back of a stationary car. Dazed and sore, we staggered out.

The driver ignored us, surveying the wreck, the probable end of his livelihood. The other driver wandered up from where he had been shunted without any show of emotion. It was dark and we were marooned on the city's outskirts. A crowd gathered in silence as I unloaded the luggage.

Thick-set men in sports shirts pushed through. I had dealt with others like them on a previous visit to India, while researching the exploits of the serial killer Charles Sobhraj. 'You must try to be more careful in our country,' one of them warned, introducing himself as a senior detective and summoning a taxi. For the second time, I paid in advance for the trip to the hotel, musing on the karma of being a tourist in India.

The statistics of life in Bombay are depressing. Over a hundred thousand inhabitants sleep, eat and give birth on the streets. Hundreds more join them each day, lured by the rags-to-riches fantasies of Hindu musicals. The rat population is estimated at seven million – but who does the counting? On Marine Drive, a huge billboard warns: 'Don't Give Alms to Extended Palms', but some beggars have no arms, much less palms, to extend.

On the magazine stands, titles like *Savvy, Femina* and *Working Women* reflect the impact of feminism. A karate black belt – once Charles Sobhraj's personal trainer – is now renowned for the popularity of his martial arts classes for women. For the first time, the law allows victims of rape to sue 'even if', at the time of the assault, they were not virgins. Men who harass women in public can be charged with 'Eve teasing'.

Accommodation is scarce, and most young adults live with their parents. I was a dinner guest at the home of a prosperous financier and a pious Hindu, who meditates at dawn and hides his light under a bushel. He finances a hospital for the poor which he does not talk about. At my urging they discussed politics ('The Sikh rebellion was CIA inspired'), the city's overcrowding ('I almost went to gaol for opposing Sanjay Gandhi's strict birth-control measures, but I can see now I was wrong'), as well as the undeniable reality of their spiritual life ('The greatest impediment to meditation is the intellect'). Until we cease to find this statement amusing, I suspect we shall never understand the Hindus.

The two grown-up children, whizz-kids in the world of advertising, fidgeted tolerantly through all this, until their turn came to prattle about the best brand of hi-fis and the hot Hollywood thrillers. I asked the son to name the biggest drawback of life in Bombay. After some thought he replied: 'I cannot buy a single record by the Kinks. Can you imagine that?'

For the city's millions, the most pressing problem is lack of space. Makeshift canopies line inner-city streets crammed with families whose water is pirated from the cisterns of public toilets. These, too, are packed to capacity; the Hiltons of homelessness.

The comparatively wealthy, like the friends I dined with, who live in a 'luxury' apartment with uncertain water supply and broken lifts, are increasingly apprehensive. Strangers squat under alcoves, cook under the staircase and defecate in the lobby, while I, the passing tourist, take refuge in a grand hotel.

The disparity is so acute that it is only endurable for a short time. The guilt of a couple of gluttonous forays into the fabled smorgasbord of the Taj Mahal Hotel gave me anorexia. The pleasure of the panoramic swimming pool was diminished by my research into the municipal equivalents, where children queued for hours and swam in a solution calculated at seventy per cent urine.

Not being Mother Theresa, I was glad when the monsoon broke and we could leave the city in search of the real India, where our optimism might be more becoming. Yes, off to the deserts of Rajasthan, with their pink cities, palaces of winds and marble, forts, castles, Maharajas and camel fairs.

I had heard about a caste of farmers who had greened the desert with their love for all things living, save anyone who harmed their sacred animal – the Blackbuck Deer. Known as the Bishnois, they were strict vegetarians who never slaughtered their livestock – in contrast to the macho caste of Rajputs, renowned for polo, pig-sticking and gin-slinging. The Bishnois had vowed long ago never to cut a green tree or even to hurt a fly, and their villages were distinguished by the profusion of lush vegetation, endangered birds and graceful herds of deer.

Due to a thriving demand for their dairy products and their skilful agronomy, the tribe was famously prosperous. In search of them, we drove west from Jaipur into the dust storm, which quelled the fury of the midday sun, if not our exasperation at the bizarre obstacles put in our way.

At a railway crossing we were gridlocked in a massive convoy at the locked gates, watching and waiting, while many men fiddled down the track with the headlights of a steam engine. To our astonishment, but not that of the locals, the train never headed our way, but backed into the distance, as the unnecessary gates swung open. The next crossing was utterly impassable, because the attendant had locked the gates and gone to a wedding.

In rocky Jodhpur, home of the riding breeches, we stayed with relatives of the Maharaja, who had built tourist huts in the gardens of their palace. The dining room was hung with the paraphernalia of colonial blood-sports and the visitors' book dated from the twenties. Understandably, the British admired the people of Rajasthan and were less concerned with subjugating them than joining the Rajputs on tiger hunts. The firm handshake, the bold gaze, the breezy humour, the forts stacked with treasure . . .

It was a Maharaja who created the first Bishnoi martyrs. In

1731, he sent his men to log a forest, for yet another palace. The largest grove, typically, circled a settlement of Bishnois. When the villagers resisted, troops were dispatched. Hundreds of Bishnois rushed to the grove, each one flinging their arms around a tree. As the first axe fell, a woman named Amrita Devi let out a cry, which later became a rallying call: 'A chopped head costs less than a felled tree.' This failed to impress the axemen. When the Maharaja visited the site at the end of the day, and saw over 300 bodies scattered and mutilated, he had a Damascus conversion, vowing to respect their beliefs. Logging in Bishnoi areas was banned henceforth.

Our cars entered the village at dawn. Scores of women in crimson skirts and bodices, with brass water-pitchers on their heads, were walking by the side of the track. Everywhere there were birds: peacocks, partridges, pigeons and Great Indian Bustards. Children smiled and waved. The walled mud and dung dwellings along spotless roads would have inspired Le Courbusier and Goudi. In contrast to the dazzling raiment of the women, the men wore white. Everything seemed beautiful, almost Biblical.

A white-turbaned man with obvious authority led me to an enclosed courtyard and offered me a silver bowl of buffalo milk. It was an auspicious day. A villager was bringing home his new bride. All the district was coming to celebrate, including a Bishnoi who was a federal member of Parliament.

About fifty men sat cross-legged under a canvas awning in a whitewashed courtyard, everyone still, with just a murmuring hum like bees in a summer garden. Their large eyes were black and bottomless. Normally, they would be toiling in the fields – today they were drinking opium. As a matter of courtesy, I joined them.

On the other side of the courtyard, the women were a turmoil of colour and sound. No drugs for them. They laughed, talked, played with the children, jewellery dangling. The oily opium was boiled with water, cooled, strained and poured from a wooden bowl into my cupped hand.

I just sat there, dreaming. Jhambaji, a shepherd born in 1451, founded this branch of Hinduism. He was first sighted in a forest, some say, being suckled by a deer. Others maintain he was an ordinary boy, shocked by ravages of a drought. When Jhambaji saw his people strip the land of its foliage to feed cattle and hunt down the antelope to feed themselves, he had a vision: humanity can only survive by living in harmony with nature, life is worth living only by letting others live.

This insight was codified into twenty-nine principles, from which the name of the tribe is derived: Bish (twenty), noi (nine). Some precepts mirror the Ten Commandments, others are more eccentric: never geld a bullock; always scatter grain for birds; be content with your lot; refrain from tobacco, marijuana, alcohol and – yes – opium.

A red limo materialized, flags flying, air conditioners whirring, and a huge man stepped out wearing Western clothes, all white – the politician. I asked about the opium eating, and he lamented it as a 'terrible vice'. The British were to blame. All the other precepts were strictly adhered to. When the politician thought I wasn't looking, he popped a lump of opium into his mouth.

Learning that I was from Australia, the village headman had just one question: How much wool is produced by a Merino? When I failed to answer it, I saw myself plummet in his esteem.

The bride and groom arrived by tractor and, with much singing and dancing, made a majestic entry into the village square. Elated by the warmth of their reception, the hospitality of the village, their opium, their idealism, we loaded our gear into the car. As far as the eye could see, there were women with pots on their heads, walking alone or in groups by the side of the road, heading for wells; hundreds of them silhouetted against the crimson clouds as we drove away ... so lost in the scene, no one lifted a lens.

Two weeks later, grumpy in the back of a cab on my way to Bombay airport, I shout at the driver, heart thumping, 'Will we make it?' 'I will pray for you, Sahib.'

At this moment, nothing could be worse than missing a flight to Sydney. Why? What's so terrible about a few extra days in India? The mood-swings are hard to explain to anyone who hasn't been there – the good times don't come lightly. You pay for them with the bad times, and baksheesh. The reason I'm running so late is that the hotel accountant had decided – mysteriously, impishly – that the signature on my credit card was not mine.

With darts and spurts and silent prayers, the sweaty taxi makes it to the plane on time. As I lug my bursting suitcase into the lounge, stuffed with hand-embroidered curtain fabric, the security chief at the airport demands that I be given a 'thorough going over'. The painstaking packing of the previous night is laid out on the departure benches for all the world to see – which it does – as I stand there in a rage. A rage that is utterly ephemeral. India casts a spell on its departing visitors – the gift of selective amnesia. Eventually, we all go back.

(*Sydney Morning Herald*)

7
My Balls in the Thresher

Click to the shears, boys . . .

1987:

Women love vasectomy, and not only because it shifts the burden of contraception. The icy, probing fingers, the blade-plunge into the genitals, the extraction of a life-giving tendril, snip, snip, snip, the toothy clamps, the scourging, the blood, the stitches, the vanquished sperm (where does it go?), the high risk of irreversibility, and the humiliating aura of a desexed tomcat, all adds up to a little consolation for the ladies. Something to even the score. 'Don't be a pipsqueak,' they sneer, 'we go through worse for a check-up.' And it's true. A routine pap smear is like *The Invasion of the Body Snatchers*. A pregnancy entices deep probings, sometimes in front of the trembling father. And not all doctors are elderly eunuchs. As our leading gynaecologist once said, with his Ferrari leer, 'I go to work where other men play.' No wonder women are thrilled at the thought of men in stirrups.

So far, I've avoided the cruellest cut, the Samurai swish of the surgical scythe, the scrotal guillotine, the castrating cleaver . . . but time is running out. Being diagnosed with low sperm-count has been a decisive argument against the need to drop my testicles into a thresher. 'Too much pot,' I would purr, putting on Billie Holiday, 'sick tadpoles, no hassle, lie back.' But this brilliant approach faltered after the birth of a daughter. 'A fluke,' I stammered, 'a tidal anomaly, a medical miracle, a sperm in a million . . .' And then came a second child; so it was back to the drawing board. In fact, I am

now lashed to the drawing board – rolling inexorably towards
the circular saw.

'Tantra,' I gasp. 'Longer orgasms than you ever thought possible.' My wife stifles a yawn. 'Deep, exhilarating, eternal . . .'
She is snoring. But I study obscure Eastern texts, late into the
celibate night. By dawn I have mastered the entire Hindu
cosmology, and probed the yin and yang of Taoism. This is
my kind of birth control – no pain, oodles of sex, and, as an
optional extra, nirvana. It's both a religion, and fun. Simple,
too. I merely withhold the ejaculation. That's it – all the rest
is detail. Tantra promises to increase frequency; and to make
me a better lover. (*Impossible*, surely, demurs an inner voice.)
Best of all, it's wonderful for women. It's like having a male
harem, all rolled up into one man, perpetually on standby,
or stand-up, and I am that man. We set out on a mystical
navigation of the Tantric way of sex; the cosmic prophylaxis.
I find that withholding ejaculation is an interesting concept,
which I am sure to get the hang of, soon.

Slash! Cut! Slice! Chop! It's life on the razor's edge. Time for
investigative journalism. 'Where do they cut, exactly?' I quiz
a group of friends. Silence. 'The lower stomach.' You mean
like appendix? My wife suggests the base of the penis. Anyone
who knows my wife is not surprised at this suggestion. Even
I suspect it's the scrotum that hits the mincer. But where? At
what point? The women look vague and the men start talking
about four-wheel drives.

I consult the *Encyclopaedia Britannica*. The duct that passes
sperm from the testes to the prostate and other reproductive
organs is the vas deferens. It is this which is cut. Does it
hurt? First, 'The scrotum is anaesthetized.' That's fine, but
why stop there? Why not a full anaesthetic? A week off
work and a private room. 'The vas deferens is isolated by
external examination.' Can you picture the scene? I mean, I
like Dr Rodney and all that, but . . . Besides, our wives are
friends. An 'incision is made over the cord, it is clamped in

two spots, and severed between clamps. The two free ends of the vas deferens are then usually cauterized to coagulate the blood .. ' Aaaarrggghhhh! I faint; dreaming of being chased across a mattress by Edward Scissorhands. Upon recovery, my determination is renewed. There must be a better way.

And there is. It's astrological birth control – as practised by ethereal neighbours. 'It's harnessing the forces of the universe,' assures Mandala, 'an inter-galactic rhythm method.' She produces zodiac maps, tidal charts, and we discuss the moon. My consciousness vibrates, the loins tingle with astral awareness. But the word 'rhythm' has triggered an alarm. Er, did it work for you, I ask? 'Almost. There was a slight hiccup.' Actually, there were four slight hiccups – all of them cute.

Now, each time my wife asks me to sharpen the carving knife, a ghastly smile plays upon her lips. Panic. 'Hey, what's so bad about coitus interruptus?' I try to look like a Brazilian gigolo, and conjure up memories of romantic nights at the drive-in. Frank Sinatra, Peggy Sue, juke boxes, uplift bras, sloshy lipstick, heavy petting . . . all of it comes rushing back, a torrid stew of abandoned step-ins and coital daring. 'I was a baby in the fifties,' she snaps, telling me about her in-law, Jedd, who had a vasectomy in the morning and was back in the office by lunchtime. Thanks, Jedd.

That night, I steal into bed with a condom. Afterwards, I purr: 'See, darling, you didn't feel a thing.'

'What's so new about that?'

Then I didn't know where to put it – I mean the condom. It's the down-side of being plumbed to a septic tank. Shivering, I stood in front of the various garbage bins, thinking of leaking landfills.

For weeks, we bicker. I show her the latest medical finding of a link between vasectomy and prostate cancer. 'That's nothing,' she replies, 'that can't be settled by the doctor's digital penetration of the rectum, once a year.'

A vasectomy leaves some men with ongoing testicular pain,

I report. A small price to pay, she argues, as Jedd suffers a relapse and is rushed back to surgery.

He will soon be walking again. My wife pushes ahead with an appointment. Further research reveals that the *Britannica* omitted a crucial detail. After carving up the vas deferens, it is actually extracted like spaghetti, yards of it, miles of it, and then hacked again. 'So the two ends won't reconnect,' said my feminist informant, reminding me that vasectomy was the preferred option for women. 'In that case, why didn't your husband have one?'

'He told me that if he did – he'd never get it up again.'

Brilliant. Genius. A crate of champagne for the husband. I rush to my wife with the same excuse. She yawns: 'It's a risk I'm prepared to take.'

Okay, I hear the bright sparks at the back – the Billings method. Great. Always carry a thermometer. Get to know your girlfriend's mucus. 'Look, darling, it's like raw egg.' The yolk or the white, dummy? 'Er, more like phlegm – hey, why are you getting out of bed?'

The fatal day draws close. When I see Dr Rodney in the street, I avert my eyes. I make furtive calls to his secretary, urging a top-up of their stocks of anaesthetic. My pyjamas are packed, in case of a 'complication'. Then we get a phonecall from Jedd's distraught wife. Something has gone wrong – she is unaccountably pregnant. I dance. I sing. Jedd's wife is crying. The vasectomy . . . 'didn't take'. I am popping champagne. My wife is furious. 'Darling,' I say, hurling a glass against the wall, 'have you heard about the female condom?' A door slams; the car skids down the drive; and we are trying a new method. Abstinence.

(*Follow Me*)

8
Brrrrmmmm... Feel That Thrust

Menopause has struck. It happened in bed as I was cruising that monument to materialism, Vanity Fair. *There was an ad for a Chrysler convertible, which . . . I read; drooling over the jaunty beast the way I once did at gatefolds (ooops). The next morning the phone rang and – cosmic coincidence – I was asked to test the latest BMW. A case of mistaken identity, no doubt, as happened to the character Boot in Evelyn Waugh's* Scoop. *The most terrifying moment was the 'training session' at BMW – trying to look like a 'rev head' – but they only wanted to show me the computerized seat controls.*

1987:

I lowered my bottom on to the bison leather seat of the BMW 535i and tapped the memory code. The seat adjusted itself to envelop me with an ergonomic caress, at the same time as the three mirrors purred into electronic realignment. A slight twirl of a knob bestowed the ideal interior temperature, confirmed on the computer screen, but only on my side of the car. A separate knob cocooned the passenger. With a deft tug, I telescopically adjusted the leather steering wheel, then checked the anti-dazzle instrument panel, as glittery and panoramic as the Concorde. I slid the BMW cassette, *Classic Dreams*, into the Dolby 'anti-theft' stereo, with its optical slide control and 'digital phase-locked loop frequency synthesizer'. Then I fed the data relating to our drive-path into the 'fourth generation on-board computer' and slid in the infra red key. So far, so good; but would I be man enough to start the engine?

Earlier, the Germanic PR voice at the end of the phone had assured me: 'There is more computer technology in this BMW than existed in the whole world forty years ago.' It can diagnose malfunctions and estimate arrival times. And this BMW probably contains more bison leather, as well, than exists in the whole world today. Which is a small price to pay for passenger comfort (there is optional electric seat heating). To possess this mighty miracle, at the cost of a country cottage, is to enter a world of high-tech fantasy, gross hedonism and sublimated sexuality.

The brochure extolls the infinite calibrations of 'pleasure to be extracted' from the car and refers lovingly to its 'side skirts' and 'adjustable thigh support'. On the highway, with unconscious *double entendre*, I boasted, 'I'll soon open her up', and to the delight of my wife, I asked if she could 'feel that thrust'.

On my first drive, I sped seventy miles into the foggy night across the Blue Mountains. My passenger, a teenage nephew, turned his seat into a *chaise-longue*, opened the sunroof (electronically, of course), tape-scanned the FM stereo, and read *Stark* by map light. When the outside temperature sank near freezing, the computer screen flickered to life, warning of ice on the road. If headlights hit the rear vision mirror – a rare event – the glass tilted automatically. There was not enough time to test the infinite permutations of the air-conditioning, but my nephew claimed that a recirculating device excluded the air from outside. 'What good is that?' I inquired. Wearily, he replied: 'In case of radioactive fallout.'

Ah, the military genius of the Hun. Under the seat was a medical kit, better stocked than most hospitals, and there's an optional airbag which inflates 'so rapidly the process is scarcely noticed while the accident is occurring'. A rechargeable torch sits in the glove-box and the infra-red key unlocks the doors and lights up the interior from a distance of five metres.

On this seventy-mile trip, only two things were missing – a radar detector and cocktail bar. I shaved half an hour off my record and thirty years off my age. Which is, I suppose, the whole point of a bright red rocket (230 km/h, max), with its cockpit like a disco, the seats smelling of a bondage parlour and the cabin as cosy as a honeymoon suite.

For the next few days, neighbours expectantly hovered in my driveway. Returned from a spin, their faces were symphonies of avarice and ecstasy. Several vowed to murder rich uncles. A visiting Buddhist monk managed to wangle a ride, emerging with the dream adline: 'So silent. It is the perfect vehicle for meditation.'

Off the highway, the car was less cocky. With one pothole, I despoiled the spoiler ('carefully contoured in a wind tunnel' it may have been, but it wasn't much use on a dirt track). Caked in mud, laden with groceries and carrying our nasty baby-seat, the BMW looked forlorn and out of place, like a gazelle in a junkyard. But with a quick scrub and a taste of the Great Western Highway, it soon perked up; turning heads, inciting envy and tempting my neighbours' wives. As for the engine, I never got around to lifting the lid. The dashboard had been challenge enough.

Is it the car of the future, as the manufacturers would have us believe? Electronically, yes. But it is also the car of the past. Behind the wheel, I felt I was reliving the Decline and Fall of the Roman Empire, so sybaritic were its trappings, so strangely decadent its conception, in an age of imminent austerity. Swift and silent, it lulled me into a sensual daydream, like a float tank; and I copped a speeding ticket. 'But it only felt like sixty,' I protested. 'Of course it did,' said the officer, flushed with admiration for the beast. If the road of excess leads to the palace of wisdom, then this is the car for the drive.

(*Follow Me*)

9
Into the Mystic

Long hair can drive men crazy, especially on a man.
When the balding network chief ordered me to get
a haircut – 'it looks bloody stupid' – which until
then I'd been planning to do, I fled from his office
and a future on the Nine network. That night at
the kitchen table, Julie Clarke and I devised a plan
for a new kind of TV show, Extra Dimensions,
which would focus on 'self growth and planetary
awareness'. The morning paper carried a report
on a conference coming to Brisbane which would
feature luminaries in the consciousness movement
– a chance to do some field work: A journey to the
Australian Transpersonal Conference.

1986:

In the large round communal building at a teachers' training
college in Brisbane, 100 people lie flat on their backs. Their eyes
are shut and they breathe slowly and deeply, trying to relax on
the brink of their 'vision quest'. This is to be a forage among
the dark untrammelled furrows of their own consciousness . . .
and I am among them.

'You are walking along a path which winds up a hill,'
intoned Dr Friedmann Wieland, as the lilt of a Kitaro ambient
tape conjured up meadows, streams, and dolphins reaching
simultaneous orgasm.

The path got higher and steeper and rougher. In my mind,
it turns into a rocky trail ascending a mountain, spiralling into
a peak. But there's an obstacle, a door – huge, forbidding,

mysterious – 'which turns out to be unlocked,' continues the voice, 'and you find you can easily push it open.' I hesitate. 'You are entering the land of our visions.' Did I really want to unlock the unknown?

The guide is dropping out, leaving us alone to face whatever lay beyond the door. Worse . . . sitting beside us is a 'partner', ready to hear all that we encounter. By now, the roundhouse is carpeted with murmurs of pluckier travellers.

Shit. What am I doing here?

On one level, the answer was easy. I had come to a festival of the unconscious. Already, an overflowing auditorium had been addressed by the superstars of self-awareness – a Jungian, a rebirther, a Tibetan Lama, a shaman, a physicist. . . The delegates surprised me. Hundreds of shrinks, of course, but I kept meeting civil servants, lawyers and doctors. ('Why are you here?' I asked a dermatologist. 'Because I'm looking for the real source of my patients' skin problems.') Weary of being labelled 'mild-mannered', a civil servant told me he was searching for the anarchist within. 'You might find the mad bomber,' I said, and he started to twitch.

There seems to be a quickening curiosity about self-transfor-mation and the New Age. For years, I have been tramping this mush in a state of poised and excitable ambivalence. Self-transformation seems possible, even necessary, and today's toolkit is shiny and expanding, but there's always the shadow of the real world, the one played out on the nightly news, savage and depressing. Maybe it's why the mystics have come down from the mountain.

So how come you're still flat on your back in the round-house?

All right, all right, let's push past the wretched door . . .

Creak, creak, I'll spare you purple prose about colonnades rimmed with stalactites on sandy shores, but I'm sorry to say that I encountered an iron-masked rider on a white horse (thanks a lot, Bergman) who took me off at a flying gallop to lay waste a city. Crash, bang, rubble in seconds. Only a small city, more like Melbourne than Manhattan, and it was fun watching the tower blocks tumble.

The journey didn't end there, fortunately, but afterwards I was reminded of a phrase from my publishing past in Sydney, which I used in public debates, that 'satire is intellectual slum clearance'. Derision was in our blood back then, not just at society, but each other. The highest form of social intercourse was the witty put-down. The wise guys were wise guys. Role models had big brains and sharp tongues, scouring the libraries for anti-social ammunition. But the spirit was mean. And as the years rolled on, the meanness showed.

Transpersonal means beyond the personal. We exist in a web of mutually conditioned relationships with each other and the natural environment. For transpersonal psychology, the central focus of health and wellbeing is *consciousness* and it claims to be making new maps of the human psyche.

The optimism of this view is greeted cynically by those reared on a concept of class struggle, atheism and paranoia. You know the sort of thing, loving 'the people' but hating that person. Yet a hundred years ago there were fierce socialists, like Edward Carpenter, who toiled in the slums wearing home-made sandals and preaching cosmic consciousness. Their ideas were radical, popular and transpersonal.

Let's accept that the Mind/Body bandwagon is laden with ratbags (there I go, the endemic squib) . . . laden with seekers prone to gaze meaningfully at teabags. So what? Nuts enhance the cake. Raising consciousness is hard work (in my case, like raising the *Titanic*) and it's natural to want the spiritual equivalent of instant coffee. Still, whenever I hear the word guru, I itch for my revolver.

Alan Watts once said that if religion is the opium of the people, then Hindus have the inside dope. But those who worship the Rolls Royce gurus show that the dopes are on the inside. It was natural for disenchanted Westerners to go

East, to where bliss is an industry – not something rumoured on the old road to Damascus. Hindu literature is full of techniques for getting high without drugs, and without gurus, but the Western fetish for superstars installs these prophets in towers of psycho-babble. That phrase may be past. Enlightenment is not about men, but about methods.

Oh what a wank, you might say, the world is hurtling to catastrophe and you're poncing on about middle-class angst.

Yes, I always wondered what Buddha would have done if the developers threatened his banyan tree, and what the Tibetans will do about the Chinese razing their forests and culture. It is precisely because the world is in such a state that politics should move from the class struggle to planetary awareness and religion from prostrating at altars to altering states. That's why I believe that to turn a deaf ear to the third eye is dumb.

Meanwhile, I'm still on the roundhouse floor. So what happened after I demolished the tower blocks of Melbourne?

The faceless horseman departed – farewell, stale vision – leaving me alone to clamber through clichés of tunnels, bastions and hillsides. It was an ascent, at least, to a jagged rim of pinnacles and beyond, to a still, circular lake, which suddenly kaleidoscoped into a vista of reflected pools . . . a plateau of mirrors . . . and then the voice, Dr Wieland bringing us all back to suburbia. But it was not yet over. We had to form groups of five. In turn, each of us was asked to wear a blindfold in front of the other four and dance the vision. Why?

Wieland believes we need different visions for different stages. If a person in retirement, say, clings to an outmoded vision, they can become a vegetable, a shrunken version of the self. Deep down, each one of us already knows the next step. Weiland aims to raise a personal crisis to the level of initiation.

If this all sounds too Jungian and precious, let me connect it with the central idea of New Management: that an organization's culture is often a more powerful medium for getting

things done than its formal structure. 'By fostering the appropriate visions, heroes, stories, myths, and rituals,' writes William
B. Joiner, 'executives can create organizational cultures with
a strong sense of shared values, ideals and purposes . . . doing
wonders for morale, productivity and customer relations.'

So let the music begin. I assisted each one in my group to
strut their stuff . . . all the time dreading my dance. What
would it be? From Satire to Sartre, a jive . . . from Psychedelia
to Psychosis, a twist . . . or maybe a rumba . . . from revolution
to revelation.

My inner journey was paltry. For several days, we had been
hearing bizarre case histories presented by Stanislav Grof,
noted author and the Scholar in Residence at the Esalen
Institute. In his opening address, 'Beyond the Brain', Grof
had given a vivid account of four kinds of transpersonal
states (or Awakenings), the fruits of thirty years' delvings,
often assisted by psychedelics.

These days Grof and his wife, Christina, find they can
induce and explore transpersonal states with controlled
breathing, evocative music and body work. Grof has built
up a controversial model of the psyche, becoming one of the
chief theoreticians of the transpersonal movement. He says
his model is virtually the same as those developed over the
centuries by various mystical traditions.

Grof talked of breaking our rigid identity (that 'skin
encapsulated ego') and of creating a feeling of oneness with
all, letting the old identity 'leak through the skin' and melt
boundaries between people . . . letting them identify with trees,
mammals, the elements, insects, even amoeba, allowing them
to tune into mythologies of which they are previously unaware,
like the Aztec heaven or an Eskimo hell . . .

Is he mad?

Transpersonalists claim that thousands of Westerners are
now reaching these exalted and demanding states, because of
the upswing in spiritual practices. The buzz term is Spiritual

Emergence. Such people are not suffering a mental disease, according to this view, but are undergoing an evolutionary growth-split.

Spiritual emergence can take many forms, of which the most common is said to be the Awakening of the Serpent Power (Kundalini). Years ago the paperbacks on yoga warned readers not to mess around with Kundalini, the metaphorical serpent which lies asleep at the base of the spine. Too late. Thousands are showing symptoms of the serpent's arousal: spasms, violent shaking, complex twisting, involuntary laughing, crying, chanting, talking in tongues, clenching jaws, diarrhoea, nausea, loss of appetite, visions, barking, howling, hissing, etc., all demonstrating a 'positive restructuring of personality'.

This is the same serpent which triggered our expulsion from the Garden of Eden, some believe, now re-emerging to lead us back. An awakening of men and women, apparently, as they once again experience unity with all life and become group-conscious. Others link the Kundalini serpent of Indian tradition with the rainbow serpent of aboriginal mythology.

Back at the roundhouse, it was time for the dance . . . the dance of my vision. One of our group bound my eyes with a perfumed scarf and the music began.

Stomp, stomp, sway, sway. The warrior stuff was easy and natural but I wanted to swirl and twirl up to the lakes. Up past the silly acid trips, pàst theosophical back-alleys, beyond oblivion, beyond all the books; beyond the eurekas of yoga, meditation, homebirth . . . higher and higher until my eyes lit up with a simple truth: that the self within is identical, in essence, to the spirit of the universe . . . and that's the reason to get up in the morning. The music is over and the blindfold removed. The four supportive women look at me oddly. And I feel great.

The conference over, we are ceremonially dismissed with a reading from St Paul to the Corinthians: '. . . so faith, hope, love abide, these three; but the greatest of these is love.' After which everyone filed through the doors . . . in search, I believe, of love's wilder shores.

The delegates will melt back to mainstream with renewed faith, content to hang out in the catacombs of academia until there's a change in the 'dominant paradigm', and then, like the Christians before them, they will suddenly seem to be everywhere.

(*Sydney Morning Herald Weekend Magagine*)

10
Egg on My Lacoste

Years later, I returned to eat at a favourite restaurant in Athens, this time as a harassed father, and it was a disaster. Toddlers despise the food their parents adore, and furiously reject the standbys offered by waiters, such as boiled eggs. The phrase which forms the title sprang from my mouth as a joke. The rest came later, when the Women's Weekly *unexpectedly asked for some observations on fatherhood.*

1990:

Before parenthood, I thought of myself as a greenroom anarchist, a tongue-for-hire drifting the world in pursuit of fun, mischief and a good tan. I managed to redefine the concept of youth, stretching it from puberty to menopause, and, between the parties, wallow in tropic solitude with paperbacks and pina coladas. Kids were something other people had, along with mortgages and manicures. Then it happened to me. No longer an empty slogan, anarchy begins each day at dawn.

'Dad, what's the difference between phlegm and vomit?' my daughter asks, as I brew the wake-up tea. 'Why did God make blow-flies?' The new baby wakes up, wanting to party in a pooey nappy, and there's a marital spat over who forgot to put the school uniform in the drier . . . the rigmarole begins of a world once despised – how did it happen?

There was a time, a golden time, on Greek islands off season, when you could live forever with your lover on tinned sardines, warm bread, Feta and retsina. Months pass, even years, and in the village square one night, with calamari and Rembetica, the music of hash and rebellion, talking, ever talking, a waiter arrives with an ice bucket of French chardonnay, unordered. He nods at a nearby table, where a plump burgher, encircled by beaming partner and jolly tots, holds up a glass, as if to say, 'Have a drink on us.' We do, my lover and I, and are altered forever – not that we know it yet. The worm of revolution has entered our souls: families can be fun.

But only sometimes. Kids today are more trouble than ever – rebellion-without-cause has regressed from high school to high chair. The latest theory is that democracy is no longer a political process, to be studied in class, but a visceral addiction, genetically implanted. Toddlers demand the same rights as oldies: to be selective about food, to have money for shopping and to 'sleep over' with a loved one.

At the age of four, my first daughter quizzed me on the meaning of 'cosmos'. A year later she asked if scientists had invented the stars. 'No, it was probably God,' replied my wife nervously. 'That's good,' said Lucy, 'because I quite like the stars.' At six, after being told to put on her sox, she turned to her mother and said, 'I've had about as much as I can take of your nonsense.'

The logic is savage. When asked to tidy her room, she said: 'Only if I can watch Gumby on TV.'

'That's blackmail, darling.'

Later, when she wanted me to make her a sandwich, I said: 'OK. But nip out and pick up the newspaper.'

'That's blackmail, Dad.'

Parental bossiness, apparently, stems from our 'jealousy of childhood'. Such emotions are in the air right now, because Lucy has a new sister.

'I love you Tootsie,' she was saying this morning, drumming with chopsticks on her sister's head. Then she put a rubber tarantula in her bassinet. Another time I heard the baby crying, and rushed to her room. Lucy announced: 'We just had a wrestle, and Tootsie won.'

A delight of fatherhood is the free advice – 'Let babies cry for half an hour without picking them up, or you'll spoil them' – often from mothers of slobs, drug addicts and murderers.

Children teach you the value of time and sex, suddenly as rare as a six-plumed bird of paradise. Spontaneity is dangerous. Late one Saturday night, heavy petting on a couch, a child walks through the door: 'Oh, a naked meeting.'

Do I miss my life of old, hopping on planes and chasing rainbows? The last time I got to a Greek island, I was heavily encumbered, reeling back from the reflection of a bag-eyed wombat with egg on his Lacoste. On Symi I met a dashing seafarer, the captain of a self-built ketch, who sailed under an anarchist flag and was bound for Rio de Janeiro. On board were a dingo, a monkey, his son, and a pair of Danish starlets. 'Come,' he said, 'bring your family – I've got wine and hash galore, and a hundred unknown harbours to explore.' The kids were keen: they called it the pirate ship, and suddenly the kindergarten timetable didn't matter a damn, yet we demurred.

For some reason we came home, back to stability, doctors, school pet-shows, piano lessons, uncles and grandparents, safety and routine. But for how long?

Recently, Lucy dictated to me a description of her 'dream world':

– No blackmail.
– Roads are made of pink clouds.
– All the flies are fairies in disguise.
– Transport is by water lilies, to be rowed.
– The scissors are made of wood.
– Instead of soap, grated flowers.

My own dream is that in a few years we'll all sail off for Eldorado in that anarchist ketch, to a roadless land of pink clouds, grated flowers and scissors made of wood.

(*Women's Weekly*)

As it happened, the pirate ship struck a rock in a storm off the coast of Egypt, and sank. The captain was rescued, but the cargo was lost – tons of Lebanese hash. Perhaps we made the right decision, after all.

11
HOWLing All the Way to the Talk Shows

The Independent *wanted a piece for their regular feature, Heroes & Villains. In my first draft I tried to be smart, and to spread Allen Ginsberg across both categories, as an exemplar of my jokey ambivalence. But no, they insisted, one or the other. I settled for 'villain', heavily ironic, but still the calls poured in from afar. How could you stab an idol in the back? Sorry, Allen, it was just a flight of fancy . . .*

1990:

I saw my wife starving, hysterical, naked, dragging herself through the kitchen, porridge splashing the floor, and her eyes desperate for a fix, I mean, to get out of the fix she was in, and for me to fix the stinking sink. The house was as cold as a frozen corpse – a fuse had blown – and a daughter was howling, howling from existential despair because she was not allowed to pierce her ears at the age of six, like all her friends. And Mummy and Daddy had failed to hire the video of *Batman*. The phone rang. It was the mechanic – yes, the clutch was fucked – a fatal implosion. We ran out of saucepans (the kitchen resembled a smelter), and I fried the fish fingers in a cake tin, which leaked. The baby leapt from the high chair, her nose gushing like Vesuvius, and I almost caught her.

Later that day, with a wife on a Valium drip and a baby interned at the house of an in-law, I noticed an excited ad for the biography of Allen Ginsberg, the American beatnik saint. Who

could forget *Howl* (1956), his famous rave – 'the best minds of
my generation destroyed by madness' – or fail to admire the way
he moved through the decades with a tambourine and a beard,
peace chants and pot, marching on the Pentagon and cleansing
himself in the Ganges? The James Dean who never died, the Easy
Rider who never dismounted, the orgy which never ended, the
joint which never stopped jumping, the streetwise gay who was
too smart to be destroyed by the madness of family life.

But beneath the saintly exterior of bliss was a villain. Playful,
well-intentioned and Buddha-loving, but a villain nevertheless.
A trickster.

Allen Ginsberg fooled a generation into thinking that being a
rebel was daring, noble and tough; sitting up in poverty and tatters,
hollow-eyed at night smoking in the supernatural darkness of
coldwater flats floating across the tops of cities contemplating jazz.
Shucks, that's easy stuff. Have you ever tried to organize a slumber
party for a seven-year-old? (Invitations, location, games, catering,
prizes, cake, tantrums, accidents, wee-wees, video rights . . .) In
the morning, beatniks don't have to make the play-lunch.

Instead, Allen served up his *Reality Sandwiches* (1963) and
hit the road – we thought it went on for ever. 'The only ones
for me are the mad ones,' wrote Jack Kerouac, 'the ones who
are mad to live, mad to talk, mad to be saved . . .' Yes, yes,
yes, we tried never to yawn or say a commonplace thing and
to burn burn burn – exploding like spiders across the stars. And
then we faltered. Bodies began floating to the shore, including
those of Kerouac himself and the mythologized driver of the
Magic Bus, not to mention a few thousand other casualties
from drink, drugs, disease and general despair. And through it
all, Allen Ginsberg prayed, partied and played his tambourine.
He was wonderful. A bearded Buddha swathed in love-beads.
An inspiration. An illusion.

People ask if I'm full of remorse for my decade as a
middle-class rebel. Sure. The biggest regret is that it wasn't
three decades. That's why I'm so jealous of Allen. He's still

howling all the way to the talk shows. Al's worried about his loyalties. He's worried about world peace. He's worried about his love affairs. I'm worried about teething.

The Beats created a cryptic mirage, one that made having a good time seem like a sacrifice. We're just going to whip down to Mexico and live in a bordello and pickle ourselves in tequila and get busted in Laredo and write best-sellers in ten minutes and live for ever in café society, fêted by Madonna. For the rest of us, now, it's a different tune, as we move from Playpower to Cold Power; from fucking the system to fixing the cistern, from ecstasy in Ibiza to ennui at the supermarket. Where has all the flour gone, gone to weevils, every one . . .

People say it gets better when the kids are teenagers, but I'm not convinced. Seasoned parents often look as if they've stepped out of shock therapy. Chastity was such a dear until her periods came, and now she spends the days shooting up, shoplifting and spitting at her mother (a true story). It only lasts a few years. The parents just sit and wait. One day Chastity will have a child of her own . . . ha!

OK, so there's still The Road. No more garbage nights. I took the family to the Red Heart of Australia, chugging through deserts and contemplating crocodiles. A yellowing copy of *Howl*, a poncho, a flute, Van Morrison cassettes and untamed wilderness in the north. It was daring, crazy, sublime . . . In the mighty gorges, I washed nappies. By the campfires bathed in moonlight, I read *Heidi* to my daughter. At midnight we caught pythons with care and fondled them under the spotlight. Surprisingly, it did the trick. The real road was better than the fantasy; *Heidi* was as moving as *Howl*. Suburbia was defeated, however briefly. And as for Ginsberg and the Beats, they became faded memories of a distant planet, a time now past. In the wild outdoors, howl is something only the dingoes do.

(Independent Magazine)

12
The Tyranny of Hip

How can you go to Goa these days when Goa has gone to the dogs?

1990:

At an alarming age, my little daughter refused to have her hair styled in a way that wasn't 'cool'. No amount of argument about naturalness or convenience could make her change her mind. She had entered the Land of Distinction, of U and non-U, in and out, hip and square, cool and uncool, groovy and straight, brill and rank – all the categories of which I was unconscious until I finished school. That was due to my late development and the late development of Australia. In 1958, *everything* was uncool.

Some groups made a fetish out of hairstyles and Holdens – like bodgies and widgies – but were themselves so non-U as to have little impact on the nation's psyche. It was the middle class which seized on foreign fads as a rebellion without tears, and without leaving home.

I spent the next thirty years trying to be hip. It was like sailing through life in the crow's nest, scanning for cultural exotica. The sighting was more to my taste than the actual experience, for which I had to be dragged ashore by fellow travellers.

Something's happening and you don't know what it is, do you, Mr Jones? No, but I was there to tell him. That's because deep down, I was Mr Jones – a nerd in velvet bell-bottoms. Anyway, it was easy to be a step ahead, because everyone else was a mile behind. And then came the entrepreneurs, the hucksters, the copy-writers.

Rock was wrested from rebels in a basement fiddling with echo-mikes, and turned into a multi-million-dollar hype, a horrendous wall of hideous sound. Grass was transformed from a dopey pastime to a cut-throat cartel of crack, corruption and tragedy. Free love moved from a group-grope to an expensive way of death. A predilection for utopia was diminished to a disco called Revolution and a hamburger at the Hard Rock Café. Bob Dylan was cited in court for beating his wife. A yen for yoga was marketed as the Festival of Mind, Body and Spirit, and meditation became a stress-reduction course at IBM.

Overnight, 'trendy' turned from being a pejorative label into a global lifestyle. And there is no escape. The former crashpads of Asia are now pulsating resorts, with *Women's Weekly* package tours and Foster's on tap. How can you go to Goa these days, when Goa has gone to the dogs?

It was in this context, with the world so incredibly hip, groovy, cool and tedious – thanks a lot, Mr Jones – that I discovered the landmark of Squaresville, a place I had always dreaded, which turned out to be paradise enough. An isthmus of serenity in a sea of schlock, only a few hours from a big city – and I'm not saying where. There are no faces daubed in fluorescent zinc, video shops or cappuccinos.

Two-parent families can still be seen coasting the roads on bicycles, their pre-teens not yet at reform school. U-turns in the main street are easy. The local pub eschews the archetype of male urinal and boasts a large, pastel dining room, reminiscent of a fifties cruise-ship, offering elegant four-course fare on the cheap. A little ferry, like an Enid Blyton tug, chugs family groups to picnic spots. After a few days here, the endemic tranquillity seeps into the soul like fine poetry, and you find yourself whistling Nat King Cole, holding hands in daylight and Being Nice to Relatives.

No buildings soar higher than the gum trees, and enough fibro shacks remain to deter the gentrifiers. But it's coming. A planned twenty-three-million-dollar resort will encroach on the public beach and park, disrupting the marine life. It includes a huge hotel and a ninety-berth marina. Ads in the prospectus say it all: strung-out guests flick through Booker-prize novels on Laura Ashley couches, as cappuccinos are frothed and the BMW is valet-parked.

How do you preserve a way of life? It's difficult to organize a demo on the theme of Stay Still. In the slow lane, there are no fast bucks. We need a new movement, to put an end to all movement. Meanwhile, it's goodbye, Squaresville. I'm glad I fell in love with you, the day before you died.

(*HQ Magazine*)

13
The Cook, the Thief, His Wife, Her Lover...and the Old Hippie

There is a fine but firm line between the forceful repudiation of a cultural artefact and the call for its prohibition, but not everyone is bright enough to see it. This piece was dashed off on the roadside while waiting for a towtruck, the morning after seeing an acclaimed film by Peter Greenaway. I felt that the director – like some of his cast – had no clothes, and so I blew my top. The reaction from readers was wild. Overnight, I had become a prig in a hippie wig.

1990:

The man is naked and in pain; pummelled by a gang of thugs. Snarling abuse, the ringleader bastes the victim with excrement, and globs it into his gob. Dogs bark, onlookers mock and a bejewelled moll surveys the hijinks. The man is urinated upon, and the toughs strut off to a fancy restaurant. Welcome to the opening of 'one of the finest movies to come out of Britain in the last decade', according to the *Guardian* critic. 'Magnificent'.

The woman is punched in the stomach by her husband, the ringleader. Another diner is kneed in the groin. A child is beaten and abducted. A kitchen hand is floored and tortured. More guests are set upon – one of them is soaked in soup and forcibly fed. The wife reappears, embroidered with bruises, and another woman is stabbed in the check with a fork. By the time the child is savaged for the second time, I flee the cinema, sensing that worse is in store.

The glossy flier brooks no dissent. 'A masterpiece of movie invention,' trumpets the reprint from the UK's *Financial Times*, which calls it 'a sort of Jacobean melodrama gone post-modernist'. People who failed to appreciate its 'greyhound sleek plot enriched with marrowbone metaphor' were drones in the 'Bank of Honourable Stupidity', and stuck with a single-figure IQ. *Blitz* magazine was more succinct: 'Sex, murder, cannibalism', it raved, 'it's all there and more . . . quality erotica.' Other critics agreed: 'breathtaking' . . . 'dazzling' . . . 'brilliant' . . . In essence, this new film by Peter Greenaway, *The Cook, The Thief, His Wife and Her Lover*, is considered a cornucopia of *multiplying subtle resonances, Biblical Allusions, frozen painterly gestures and mobile revelations* . . . As I slunk homewards, a wayward cipher at the Bank of Stupidity, I wondered who was the craziest: the Film-maker, His Critics, Our Culture or Me?

At core is a paradox. Our generation spent its formative years fighting for freedom of expression. We had trials, demos, an alternative press, pirate radio, sit-ins, the burning of bras and the unbanning of books. An era which began with the liberation of *Lady Chatterley's Lover* went on to canonize the Sex Pistols. Perhaps it's because we put so much energy into the defence of freedom that it goes against the grain to pass judgement on anything obnoxious, especially if it is deft, daring or unusual. With a tolerant shrug, we move from a Robert Mapplethorpe 'masterpiece' of a bum-encased bullwhip, to a pop video of Alice Cooper on a bed of nails, wielding his whip on a steamy nymph. And who dare deride, with the censorship lobby still twitching in the wings?

We live in a post-modernist Valhalla, where negative judgement is considered uncool. Criticism is complicated by the panache and technical wizardry of these dark auteurs, whose output is powerful, erotic and nasty. The meanness of spirit stays in the brain like a drug, a Largactil of the soul. Again and again we are lured back to Greenawayish feats with demented gangsters, witnessing acts of sadistic brutality. Why do we return, when our presence is an act of collusion?

'But the music,' a friend said, when I quizzed her about the ending of *The Cook, etc.*, 'wasn't it wonderful?' I suppose so. Notable too were the costumes, the 'painterly' colours, the direction, the acting, the mood. But I wanted to know the fate of Alan Howard, the bookish adulterer. His death was so gruesome, she explained, that she would rather not discuss it – anyway, the lover was finally cooked and served for dinner. Yum yum. Surely, if life is too short to stuff mushrooms, then it's too short by half to watch people stuffing themselves and then eating their rivals. OK, so we appreciate that the director is gifted, but what is he saying? What is the film's insight into the human condition? When the end credits roll, what is the audience left with?

What we are left with is this – a load of the same substance that was smeared on the nude in the beginning – with a difference. Unlike the victim, viewers do not have the benefit of a hose-down.

In art, as in life, this is not the time for nihilism, sadism or spiritual defilement. Most of us are aware that the world is top-heavy with gangsters and that barbarity is many-headed. But with environmental disruption facing each human on Earth – some say a cataclysm – the time is urgent for cleansing the atmosphere; and ridding the soil and the sea from pollutants and poisons. This also applies to our culture. As surely as toxic residues kill the fish and the fowl, so the gangrenous sludge of a bastardized intelligentsia kills our spirit. It is renewal and valour that is needed now, honour and optimism, not the sordid excesses of lionized shock-addicts.

How to regain our sense of discrimination? Big bucks are spent on analysing the waterways and rainforests, but who is evaluating the messages of media? Stars jump up and down over what's sprayed on the veggies, and are cheerfully oblivious to what's spliced on to celluloid. People are obsessed with what they put in their mouths, and are seemingly indifferent to what they store in their psyches. Sure, let's clean up the garbage in Antarctica, but what of the garbage in our living-rooms? This is not to seek a revival of censorship, imposed from the top, but to renounce our reticence for what it is – a hangover from a long-lost era of uptightness.

Stage, TV, cinema, books and magazines – what is their impact on society; and how do they influence our values and attitudes? Is their message reflective, as so many claim, or can they foster pestilence? A quarter of a century has passed since I cheered for the right of Lenny Bruce to swear on stage, but does that mean I must lift a finger to help the hate-radio Alf Garnetts to stoke up prejudice against women, gays and minorities? The claim to be satirizing bigotry is often a mask for indulging it.

When you sit around the kitchen with friends, some of them veterans of censorship wars, they will admit to being perturbed by what confronts children on TV, but are too ambivalent to act. Thirty years of libertarianism is not a good grounding for phoning the ABC – as my wife did – to protest the showing of vivid Aztec torture rituals on a Sunday morning.

At Easter, I took a friend's child to the Royal Agricultural Show, where, of course, shopping, shopping, shopping has long ago crushed the ambience of prize fruit, feathers and furs. All the desires of this dainty princess focused on three showbags: police paraphernalia, army weaponry and Ninja Turtle killing tools. When the contents were laid out in the living-room, it was like a training camp for the Khmer Rouge. Appropriately, the first pair of handcuffs slipped on by this nine-year-old could not be unlocked. Whatever the forces which drove her to convert the nursery into a dungeon, it is time to admit reservations about the shape of our culture. A critical vacuum is unfair to the future.

It is like watching something die, something more precious than a lake or a mountain stream.

Every day, a new example. Perhaps it is a little thing, as with the start of a terminal illness. The latest fashion is footie: a player is tackled and before he can rise to play the ball, an opponent gives his face a good grind in the dust. And then puts in the boot. So Jacobean. So post-modern.

Film and video have reached such levels of sophistication that our critical sensibilities are overwhelmed; numbed and inoperative. Dazzled by technique, we ignore the content. In fact, the only content which registers is the technique. Alone in a darkened space, we're no match for the boffins from Special FX, the tinsel-town hype, computer marketing and the whizz-bang reviews. But now that we are finally learning to recycle our trash, what about pre-cycling our entertainment?

Is it life-enhancing, or life-degrading? Does it glorify what it pretends to condemn? Is it oriented towards a solution, or does it overly magnify the problem, in order to thrill and to gild the bottom line? Is it defeatist, ignoble, sadistic; or is it empowering, illuminating, honourable? If these questions sound fuddy-duddy, it shows how far we have drifted from a sense of purpose, and a shared inclination to evolve. Beware the triumph of misfits with brains.

The Jungian psychologist James Hillman, in a wonderful Schumacher Lecture, presented the problem of 'psychic numbing' against a background of demonic archetypes and spurned Gods, and his conclusion is relevant. Hillman suggests the 'shocking possibility' that the more we shrink away from the world and into our private functions, focusing on to the interior psyche, the more we contribute to the decay of civilization. 'Reawakening the sense of soul in the world,' he believes, 'goes hand in hand with an aesthetic response – the sense of beauty and ugliness – to each and everything, and this in turn requires trusting the emotions of desire, outrage, fear and shame . . .' Outrage, in particular, has a social function, responding to moral and aesthetic atrocities, and leading us into the fray . . .

According to a report in the *Herald* (15 May 1990) a dozen

children aged between four and eight were recently treated in
Cairns Hospital for sexually transmitted diseases. They came
from the Kowanyama community on Cape York Peninsula.
In another remote aboriginal community, 'men had forced
children as young as seven to engage in acts depicted in
pornographic videos'. Elsewhere, a five-year-old boy suffered
internal injuries after older boys had tried to emulate a porno
scene. And when a ten-year-old boy was sexually assaulted,
the first question asked by the white police, apparently, was
whether he enjoyed it.

The source of this nightmarish report was attributed to a
consultant to the Prime Minister's Department, who said that
acts of brutality were increasing with the wider availability
of videos. 'Because it's on film,' she explained, 'it must be
somehow normal, so it's all right to go out and do it.'
Exactly. This is an extreme and tragic case of what many
of us are suffering, unconsciously or otherwise. A loss of our
sense of normality. If the video player at Kowanyama is ever
loaded with a tape of *The Cook, etc.*, then it's only a matter of
time before victims are admitted to hospital. Coprophilia and
cannibalism will finally have reached our indigenous heartland,
courtesy of one of the finest films to come out of Britain in the
last decade.

(*Sydney Morning Herald*)

Postscript

The outpouring of letters showed that many had felt the same
way, but were previously too timid to express an opinion for
fear of being uncool. On the other hand, star-struck academics
demanded my head on a platter. As I pointed out at the time,
such people are mild-mannered pacifists who hold secure jobs
and wouldn't dream of buying a Big Mac, spanking their kids
or renovating with rainforest timbers. Deep down, however,

they feel part of themselves denied, and wish to honour this self in their savourings of popular culture. Their inner serial killer. Wading through blood and gore makes them feel young and alive, just as they felt in the sixties, when they read about anti-war demos and sang protest songs under the shower. Today, mainstream media-culture thrives on pseudo subversion – often orchestrated by corporate hard-hats – who are happy to slaughter sacred cows. As long as it's not the cow of conspicuous consumption.

14
Blowing in the Mind

His senses have been stripped, his hands can't feel
to grip, his toes too numb to step . . . Wait only for
my boot-heels to be wanderin' . . . into the foyer.
A night with Old man Dylan.

1992:

The reports of his performance were so damning that I didn't want to see Bob Dylan. Let him live in memory at the Isle of Wight, I told myself, where he shimmered in a cream suit while half a million of us rolled around in the mud pretending to have an orgy for *News of the World*. In Sydney, apparently, he stared at the floor and croaked out the chestnuts in a whiney falsetto.

But to my surprise, I found myself on a city-bound train in the April twilight, heading down from the mountains to meet friends at the State Theatre, braced for disappointment. How tedious the reflection in the window; a greying gent with baggy eyes and a briefcase on his lap. In the press, yet another critic dismissed Dylan as a burnt-out shell going through his geriatric motions . . .

The foyer was packed and the crowd was young. And not so young. Men in pinstripes and women in black satin and pearls were dotted among the throng of tie-dyed teenagers. With its ornate, gilded ceilings and rococo mouldings, the theatre is a throwback to Regency gothic. As a child, I was bussed here with the rest of the school to see newsreels of Queen Elizabeth's Coronation. Now, instead of Her Majesty's portrait gracing the walls, were the stark warnings against cameras, videos and tape recorders. To the strains of a warm-up band, we boozed in a velvet alcove, catching the reminiscences rising from the buzz – 'When I first heard "Mr Tambourine Man",' recalled a roadie-type in wispy dreadlocks, 'I was a jackeroo on a pig farm. It changed my life.' A museum piece veered my way with a joint, which I greedily inhaled.

The next thing I remember, as we surged through the doors to the stalls, was a security guard asking me to open my attaché case, absurdly secured with a combination lock.

'You open it, darling,' I said to my companion. 'It's too dark for me to read the numbers.'

'What *are* the numbers?'

Oh, shit, 'Er, try 374 – no, 287 – maybe . . .' People jostled behind, as the eyes of the guard narrowed. It was too absurd. Did I look like a bootlegger? Giggles in the queue. The lights dimmed, the guard shrugged and I melted into the front stalls, feeling eighteen, guilty and reckless.

Next to me sat a boy of high-school age, and I asked if he knew much about Dylan.

'Oh, sure. I've got twelve of his forty-two albums.'

He started to rattle off song titles in chronological order, linking the lyrics with key events in Dylan's career, and summarizing the stance of each album – his friends in the adjacent seats fleshing out details.

On the PA: 'Ladies and gentlemen, Columbia recording star, Bob Dylan.' Thunderous applause and off he went . . . right off.

The first song was incomprehensible, and the wiry, bow-legged figure on centre stage had the look of an elderly Jewish tailor. His weariness amazed me. Did it matter? Medically, he was alive, and the band was tight. This was a legend – a Caruso on his last legs – and the crowd was cosy and forgiving. The third song evoked his classic 'Just Like a Woman' . . . 'but she breaks just like a little girl', without any melodic resemblance to the original. The bald guy on my left was devastated. He stood

up, hissed and shook his fist: 'Infanticide . . . infanticide . . .'
Others bopped to the rhythm of the new interpretation. Or
was it annihilation?

Unknown songs were interspersed with evergreens, which
were murdered before our ears. And who could blame him?
How could anyone sing the same songs in the same way, year
after year, apart from Chuck Berry? His cheeks tear-stained,
the bald accuser shuffled to the exit.

Bob loosened up, overcoming the impression that this was
his début. After 'All Along the Watchtower', I slipped out to
the foyer and found a miniature Woodstock. Sequin-shawled
mamas under smoky lights reliving old arguments about the
meaning of 'Sad Eyed Lady of the Lowlands'. A folkie with
a goatee stared moodily at the chandeliers, too moved by his
memories to sit close to their source. And who *was* Bob Dylan;
this jaded genius who had sagged under the weight of his own
reputation?

'Wow, I saw him last week in Melbourne,' muttered a
leathery fan in the adjoining urinal, 'and he really lost it with
"The Times They Are A Changing". Amazing.'

He recalled his first Dylan experience. 'Sixty-six at the Sydney
stadium on a revolving stage,' he said, pulling from his jacket a
grotesque joint, like a Fabulous Freak Brother: 'Sumatran heads
– no tobacco.' As I inhaled, a leathery gang materialized and the
dope fiend tensed. 'Relax man,' I said, reverting to hippyspeak,
'this is what it's supposed to be all about.'

The others chimed, 'Right on,' and the male bonding
resumed.

'Dylan thinks he caused the counter-culture single-handed,'
remarked a gnome-like hipster, 'which is why he went so
paranoid, but he's wrong. We caused him.'

Back in my seat, or, rather, levitating above it, the unknown
lead guitar was supersonically pounding away until the crowd
caught fire. Dylan, his eyes finally flickering, fanned the flames
. . . 'I Don't Want to Work on Maggie's Farm No More'.

The schoolboy climbed on his seat and shook his hips, his eyes shining, only to be subdued by the dirge-like version of 'Desolation Row'.

Long ago, when we were trying to break from the mainstream, Dylan lifted the game. If he's on our side, we said, not fully understanding his lyrics, but sensing their depth, it was the only side to be on.

His protest was poignant – 'Hard Rain', 'God on Our Side', 'Blowing in the Wind' – but not the sole source of his spell. The mystery lyrics tapped the collective unconscious, the jewels and binoculars hanging from the head of a mule, or an 'Einstein disguised as Robin Hood with his memories in a trunk' – images which remain potent and mad.

Nowadays, maybe the Freewheelin' Bob on Highway 61 has turned into the forlorn Mr Zimmerman in the wrong hotel suite, shrouded in contractual obligations and beset by screwballs and gold-diggers. For a few fleeting moments, pumping up the volume in his grimy leathers, he inflamed the crowd. The more it roared, the more alive he became, until he hurled his cowboy hat to the wings: 'Come fathers and mothers throughout the land . . . don't criticize what you can't understand . . .' This turbo rock version put new life into the old anthem, freeing it of nostalgia, and whetting anew our desire for fun, marijuana and social reform . . .

OK, so we're not all living in communes writing poetry and making mischief, but thirty years of Dylan's genius is proof of life beyond MTV, and a reminder of dreams held dear.

As an encore, Dylan sang alone under a spot with an acoustic guitar, a traditional folksong, bringing it all back home, back to the Village Vanguard, back to his roots. And as we poured through the exit, unwise in our times, but wild in our hopes, we too had come full circle, back to our own beginnings. For a short time, the footpath smelt of Morocco.

(Unpublished)

15
To the Tip! To the Tip!

*Bruce offered to arrange two four-wheel drives
to be waiting at Cairns in far-north Queensland
where we could stock up with food and a tent.
'Bring the kids,' he said, 'and see Cape York before
it's fucked by the space port.' So we did. The point
of the safari was to test the vehicles . . . and us.*

1991:

The guidebook to the Cape was discouraging – redolent
with impassable roads, unstoppable sandflies, unswimmable
beaches and risks that demanded welding equipment. Ex-
hausted, for various reasons, I dreamt of a villa on the
Mediterranean. But the trip to the tip was in motion – cars
shipped, gear hired – and there was no escape. Anyway, the
motoring editor had once camped on a Greek beach with my
wife, and she said he was fun.

In all, we were ten. Six children, ranging in age from one
to fourteen, and two sets of parents. By the time we reached
Cooktown, the families had mastered each other's names, as
well as the entire musical soundtrack of *The Little Mermaid*.
The silver Nissan Patrol and the shiny black Toyota Landcruiser
(twin-tanked and turbo-powered) both drew admiring glances
as we topped up for the trek ahead. Bruce lashed a jerry-can
to the roo bar of the Nissan, and then confided to me that
he had fitted us both up with 'wenches'. Ah, the sixties
revisited, I mused, thrilled by his spunk. And the wenches like
being oiled, he confided, to heighten performance. Mmmm.
Much later, however, when he began to talk longingly of

flashing his welding equipment, I realized he was referring to winches.

The four-wheelers were fitted with CB radios, enabling various members of the Bruce family, cruising close in front, to keep us fully informed of dips in the road, the passing of wild pigs and the oncoming trucks. As the driver of the second vehicle, I realized this device was essential, for anyone blind. As we probed deeper into the North, Bruce was warned darkly of 'salties', those fierce and fast-breeding crocs which would encircle our tents at night and perhaps eat our baby.

We arrived at Laura in the early afternoon, dusty and cranky, and set up camp beside the river. Our tent, hired in Cairns, was designed for idiots and shot up in seconds with a single pole. The Bruce tent was an elaborate affair, consisting of a dozen metal poles, and as twilight descended he was still juggling and cursing. I lit the fire as Sonia – Bruce's wife – rummaged about in a box for a lamp. 'I should warn you,' she whispered, 'that my husband is totally impractical.' At that point, their tent came crashing down.

Soon the sausages sizzled and the salad was tossed. From now on, there would be no more fresh food until Bamaga, apart from the barramundi that Bruce would haul from the rivers. His tackle was spectacular. Our gas lamp was faulty and flickered aimlessly as the kids stood around holding dim torches and whining about the lack of a bench-top and bickering over the dollops of tomato sauce. (Originally, the food-box was to double as a table, until it was discovered that we could not, at the same time, eat off it and have access to it.) It drizzled and we shooed the children into their sleeping-bags. I stoked the fire and went for a walk, planning to end the first tropical night by staring moodily into its embers, a tequila in hand. When I stumbled back to the site, Bruce was pouring water into the ashes, as Sonia apologized: 'He's Aquarius – a water sign.'

The morning was hell. Damp ground, dirty dishes, a faulty stove. Being a fire sign, I charged about with an axe.

The children moaned about the meagre breakfast, each one demanding a favourite cereal, which was unavailable. Instead, Sonia brewed a blend of raw oats and warm water, which she described as 'instant porridge'. They loved it, except for one little girl, who insisted on fish fingers. The porridge tasted like Clag.

When the sun flickered through the clouds, the children swam in the river, and the grown-ups hiked a rocky trail to view the Aboriginal cave paintings. The tropical greenery was speckled with the bright yellows of butterflies and kapok flowers. Pandanus palms guarded the sacred galleries, which were ochred with images of emus, brolgas, jabirus, serpents and sea slugs. Floating on cliffs were the famous Quinkans, or spirit figures, mostly images of men with stunning erections. The suggestion that these are linked with ancient rituals of sorcery is credible, seeing these hard-ons are maintained in perpetuity.

At the Laura pub, I thanked the owner for having directed us to our riverside camp. 'See the crocs?' he asked. An outback joke, no doubt, although during ablutions I had noticed the bubbles. 'You wouldn't have sent us there if there were,' I replied. 'Sure I would, but we never tell visitors about the crocs till afterwards. It spoils their swim.' Not to worry – these crocs were 'freshies', almost pets. The look on the faces of the children, as they were told this story, made it all worthwhile.

Onwards, to where the forests thickened and the rivers deepened. At the end of an obscure trail north of Coen, we found a spot by the mighty Wenlock. This time, however, the Bruce tent went up in less than an hour. As he heaved his swags from the back of the Landcruiser, the reason for our shortage of space became clear. The Bruce swags had been hand-crafted by Nissan, and derived from the original honeymoon futons of the Japanese royal family. Each of them could have hosted the entire party, not to mention the winches. As I unfolded my disposal-store groundsheet, I was unable to suppress my

envious sneer: 'People sleep cosy in the land of payola.' Bruce
headed downstream with his fishing tackle, and Sonia took me
aside to announce: 'As a feminist, I choose not to cook.'

The 'Oz Tours' truck was the first to arrive and encircle
our camp, its members stringing up their washing. Then came
an armoured bus, a Unimog. Soon the sandy banks of this
faraway waterway were clogged with field kitchens . . .
and froth. The women shampooed their hair like they were
auditioning for *South Pacific*, and the men grimly scrubbed
thongs. It didn't stop the barra from jumping. The tour-group
leaders brandished their magnificent catches, and we all waited
for Bruce. His wife said: 'Heat the water for instant pasta, just
in case.'

At night, the bush came alive with the sound of Midnight
Oil. Chewing on pasta, the children stared bitterly at the
array of delicacies served by the brightly lit kitchens of the
tour groups. Our campsite atmosphere was one of whining
and dining. Afterwards, with deficient lighting, there was
nothing else to do but steal into our tents and listen to the
sounds of escalating merriment. Bruce was a teetotaller. In the
morning, there was the joy of washing up. In a grey drizzle, the
group-tourists trudged through our camp with shovels. Bruce
spoke movingly of the bandicoots that would soon sniff out
their loo-paper and strew it like streamers through the forest.
We pressed on.

The road dwindled to a one-lane track, the bulldust caked our
souls, and the children lapsed into despondency. This was cold
turkey. No shops for days. They began to hallucinate Kentucky
Fried Chickens. 'Where are we going?' they kept asking. 'Why
are we here?' It was a good question. 'We're going to the tip,'
said Bruce, in the gruff voice he adopted for everyone under
forty. A little girl muttered, 'It's a long way to go to dump
rubbish.' Not that kind of tip, we explained, we're going to
the tip of Australia, the pointy bit at the very top.

The convoy reached Cockatoo Creek, a deep, hazardous

crossing with mushy banks, churned up by previous daredevils. Bruce leapt from the Toyota, his eyes ablaze, and began to oil the winches. He strode into the torrent, the waters lapping the Swiss army knife strapped to his waist. On both banks we found lots of other Bruces, all survivors of the crossing and keen to give advice.

There was talk about torque and much ado about diff locks, gear ratios, clutch fans. This was my land. These were my people. And I didn't know what they were talking about. It was like a pit stop at Le Mans.

The women and children waded across, but my baby was left strapped in the car seat. I nudged the Patrol into the rapids and the water washed over the bonnet. With incredible aplomb, I switched on the wipers and floored the throttle. 'Piece of piss,' I drawled to myself, and spat out the window, forgetting it was closed. The baby cried. The jerry can fell off. The wheels slipped, but I held her steady. As I roared up the opposite bank, a snarl curling my lips to impress the onlooking ockers, I hit a boulder. The Patrol stalled and slid backwards towards the angry torrent, now, in my mind, bubbling with crocs. The crowd hissed their derision and shouted conflicting advice. The baby screamed. I tried again. On the fifth go, after a few more whacks on the rock, I finally coaxed the Patrol to the top. The children gazed at me with heartfelt contempt, and Bruce assisted me out of the driver's seat. 'Not a bad try for a city slicker,' he said. 'Next time we'll lock it into four-wheel drive.' Everyone laughed, including the kookaburras.

North to Bamaga, the town at the top; an Aboriginal settlement on a palm-fringed coast. The kids pigged out on the Chiko Rolls and I asked about swimming. The marine stingers, at last, had moved on, and the sea was too clear for us hardened adventurers to care about crocs. As I was about to toe the brine, a shopkeeper cautioned me about the toadfish, allegedly huge: 'Yesterday, one of them took a nip at a boy's foot.'

'Is he OK?' I asked, undeterred.

'He won't walk again,' she revealed kindly. 'It took off his heel.'

We set up tents near the beach, sweating under the scorching sun, the sea looking unbearably turquoise. For a Sydneysider, accustomed to beaches that are unswimmable because of pollution, there was some novelty in being unable to swim because of the threat of dismemberment. Some of the children groaned on the sand with stomach pains, while others amused themselves in the lavatories, catching frogs. That night I sat on the beach, succumbing to Fourex fever, and planning our southern route to escape. Later I learned of another man who had spent a night on the same beach, in the same spot, and was never seen again. But they did find his thongs.

The water beneath the Bamaga jetty was silver with fish. As fast as they could lower their lines, everyone was hauling them out of the water. Bruce cast his rod and the line spun elegantly around a pole. That night we dined on take-away sausages-on-a-stick.

To the tip! To the tip! The rainforest changed from tropical to sub-equatorial and the track got tougher. Near the end of the road, we started to enjoy it. On the seventh attempt, a Bruce damper, while still burnt on the crust, was veering towards edibility. Sonia and I found a shared taste for Scrabble and wine. The children, who were looking golden and tough, had stopped pining for Coco Pops. At remote waterholes, they hurled themselves off cliffs, like Sheena and Tarzan. The runny noses had dried up and there was a mounting lust for bush tucker. By campfires, they invented horror stories and forgot about video games. In a few more months, they might have started to help with the washing up.

Filthy and starving, we checked into the Cape York Wilderness Lodge, a laid-back oasis of upmarket luxury tucked in the rainforest, with quolls strolling through the dining-room and a pool which was the only safe place to swim for a thousand miles. Our awareness that a local group of Aborigines had plans to purchase the place and pull it down only added to the guilty enjoyment of plumbing, fresh food and soft beds.

The naturalist-in-residence, bearded, khaki-shorted and radiating passion for all things that creep, offered to show us the nightlife, so the families piled into the Landcruiser, pressed a button that opened the sunroof, turned on the spotlights and cruised out into an enchanted world . . . the jungle at night.

We were waiting for what the naturalist called an 'activity period', a short phase of the moon which stimulates creatures great and small to leave their nooks and take a turn out in the limelight, where we could blast them with a flash. Wild pigs thundered past, miniature possums tiptoed through fronds, and every few kilometres we stopped and pointed a spotlight while the naturalist dashed out and swept up a stick in a bag. I thought it was a mysterious ecological ritual, until one of the sticks reared its head.

'Ah, a venomous blackie,' he enthused. 'The deadly bugger. I've been after one of those.' We should all learn to love snakes, he said. These would be kept for a few days, for the education of tourists, and then returned to the same spot they were captured. As the wriggling sacks piled up in the back seat, the children were as silent as owls.

The final few hundred metres of mainland was a rocky, winding trail, which overlooked the rainforest, and a spectacular curve of endless white beach lapped by a sea that was dotted with islands. On a rock splashed by a terrifying current, a small sign stated that we had made it to the northernmost point, and we gazed across the Torres Straits towards Papua New Guinea. As elsewhere in this impenetrable wilderness, a crowd soon gathered. But the look on the faces was different. It was holy. A man on crutches, with his leg in a cast, staggered into view.

Yes, this was a sacred site. The beginning of Australia and the end of a journey. I glanced around for totems of significance, and was not disappointed. Symbols of nationhood had been discarded by earlier explorers; a bleached can of Fourex and a faded thong. Our children's vision of the northmost point of Australia had not been far off. The tip was a tip.

(HQ Magazine)

16
The Divided Self at Desert Storm

In 1990, when the Gulf War was unleashed against 'Sodom' Hussein, the West danced on his grave, forgetting, inevitably, that it was bound to be the grave of his subjects. The phoney deadlines – 'Withdraw by January 15!' – the posturing generals and the swaggerings of the media all recalled the dark days of napalming villages in South East Asia, and there was barely a peep of protest. This was mine.

1990:

If this war is so just, as I keep being told, then why the pain in my gut; a sense of foreboding and shame?

BRAIN: You're an ageing hippie peacenik, scarred by Vietnam, and fuelled by hatred of America.

GUT: Hey! I'm Australian. To hate America would be to hate my own culture – or about 90 per cent of it. But US foreign policy has always been tough, brutal . . .

BRAIN: Oh, here we go. Bay of Pigs, Vietnam, Chile, Nicaragua, El Salvador . . .

GUT: A decade of death squads, US funded.

BRAIN: The Gulf is different. The UN has sanctioned military action.

GUT: Only to kick out Iraqi troops from Kuwait. How come we're slaughtering civilians in Baghdad and Basra?

BRAIN: What a dreamer. You've got to stop enemy supply lines. Pinpoint bombing; surgical strikes. Smash communications, bridges . . .

GUT: So how do citizens get to market? What are families eating? Where are they shitting? How do they sleep? No fuel, no water, no medicines – children's limbs hacked off in makeshift hospitals, without anaesthetics. If conditions in Basra applied to any jail in the world, it would be condemned as cruel and inhuman. So what have they done, these people of Iraq, to deserve this hell?

BRAIN: It's the unavoidable price of fighting a tyrant. The precision of the bombing is breathtaking – have you seen the media briefings?

GUT: Yeah. War, lies and video-tape. The Generals hold copyright, so we don't get to see the flattening of the powdered milk factories, the schools, the apartment blocks.

BRAIN: Those Baghdad butchers are putting their guns on suburban rooftops.

GUT: What else is left standing? Baghdad and Basra are being wiped out. Its people are being subjected to torture by remote control; day after bloody day. It's turning into a Dresden, but no one dares says it . . .

BRAIN: Crap. In Dresden, the murder of civilians was intentional, part of the plan to demoralize the enemy. It is not part of the intention to kill Iraqis.

GUT: Oh? So it's only manslaughter . . . on a mass scale; collateral carnage. No doubt the absence of intention is a comfort to the sick and the maimed.

BRAIN: I grant you that innocents are getting killed. What about the Kurds – poison gas, chemicals, yuk!

GUT: Abominable. Just like the fuel-air bombs we're planning to drop on the Republican Guard; only our chemical is petrol. And the Kurds in Syria and Turkey feel just as tyrannized as their brethren in Iraq. Turkish Kurds are forbidden to speak their own language.

BRAIN: Hasn't it sunk in? Saddam Hussein is a Hitler. But what do you think was going on in Kuwait? Pillage, torture. Babies hurled from their cribs . . .

GUT: Ha! That's the report that reduced President Bush to tears the night before he sent in the troops – and it's now been found to be false.

BRAIN: In the long run, not confronting Hussein would be worse. After Kuwait, then what? Saudi Arabia . . . Appeasement stinks. The lesson of history supports the White House.

GUT: The lesson of war is that it's always a chain reaction; the psychological equivalent to nuclear fission. The invasion of Kuwait may have been wrong, but the territorial claim is not the aberration of a madman. In June 1961, only six days after Britain formally recognized the sheikdom's independence, the Iraqi Prime Minister claimed Kuwait as an integral part of his own country. (Both had been part of the Ottoman Empire.) Ethnically, geographically and socially, Kuwait and Iraq were one country, it was argued, which had been arbitrarily divided by Britain.

BRAIN. Sssshhh! I'm the brain around here. That sounds like Iraqi propaganda.

GUT: It's direct from the *Encyclopaedia Britannica*. What's the urgent rush to kill the people of Iraq with the latest high-tech weaponry? How come there was no serious or prolonged attempt to apply pressures by other means? What was so magical about 15 January?

BRAIN: Without a deadline, there was no pressure for Iraq to pull out.

GUT: The deadline boxed us in; an old-fashioned colonial bully-boy tactic. Open your eyes, Brain. The speed of the attack, the intensity of the bombardment, the manipulation of the media, the over-stepping of the UN objective, the demonization of 'Sodom' Hussein – all this – in the 1990s – is unacceptable. Especially from nations claiming to be civilized.

BRAIN: You're so wrong, as is demonstrated by the loneliness of your position. This is a just war. A shared war. It is a chance, once for all, to stand up to tyranny and say – enough! No more Tibets, no more Timors . . .

GUT: And no more Tiananmen Squares?

BRAIN: Fool. That's an internal matter.

GUT: As is Kuwait; to millions of Iraqis. No more Grenadas, no more Panamas?

BRAIN: The UN is fully backing the Coalition.

GUT: This is good and honourable; like all the UN resolutions – over a hundred of them – which condemn the Israeli annexation of Arab territories.

BRAIN: Are you anti-Semitic?

GUT: I'm pro-planet. As we accelerate towards the Third Millennium, with the environment in tatters, and our consumer-fix still unplacated, the war is a disaster we could have avoided. A great ethical setback – a triumph of military mentality. Desert Storm is a mean-spirited operation; full of lies and cruelty. And the end is unforeseen.

BRAIN: You're just a dopey hippie peacenik.

GUT: In years to come, President Bush will be seen for what he is – a war criminal.

BRAIN: Stop. I've got a headache.

(*The Australian*)

17
Leper Rapes Truth

I love it when columnists fling up their hands and cry, 'Why is everything so bad?' As a former editor, that's my reaction whenever I walk into a newsagent's. Occasionally, I bump into the guilty publishers and ask the same question, ever so politely. Their glance is cutting, their tone is withering: you're past it. This is what the punters want. Is it?

1993:

When a human penis was recently found on the beach at Bermagui, a serene town on the south coast of NSW, I realized something irreparable and mysterious had happened. Not just to the owner of the organ, but to the soul of the nation. Like in the movie, *Blue Velvet*, when the disembodied ear was discovered and Tidy Town was exposed as a hotbed of corruption, S & M and child abuse. In Bermagui, the woman who found the penis took it to the police station, where investigations are proceeding. Meanwhile, I search the debris of the nation's psyche for clues . . .

At the same time as the intriguing flotsam was being scooped from the sands, the managing director of Australian Consolidated Press (ACP), Richard Walsh, issued a statement. His company had acquired a new title, a famous weekly newspaper, to be launched in the new year. Wonderful. My heart soared. How weary I had grown of the staple newsagent fare, *Wanker's World*, *Ocker Auto* and *Thrill Kill Replays*. Perhaps ACP had acquired the *Times Literary Supplement*. But no, the company was thrusting further 'downmarket', further than ever thought possible. Its new title was the *National Enquirer*.

As grim as the news was, at least it solved the mystery of the Bermagui penis. The landing on our shores of foreign objects is part of feedback between popular culture and human behaviour. For the *National Enquirer* to flourish, we must all start behaving like its headlines; dressing up as Elvis, partying with extra-terrestrials. It's not 'serious journalism', admits Walsh, my old friend, 'it's entertainment journalism'. In this country, nothing is more serious than entertainment.

Years ago, when I first saw the *National Enquirer* in a US supermarket, its headline read: LEPER RAPES VIRGIN/GIVES BIRTH TO MONSTER BABY. Try to imagine the picture of a two-headed foetus . . . and then how a leper might feel. In the cutting-edge terminology of the twenty-first century, Richard describes such headlines as 'jazzy'. I'll try and be jazzy and say how I feel about a homegrown *National Enquirer*: PACKER FUCKS OZ/GIVES BIRTH TO MONSTER TABLOID. For the Bermagui story, the jazzy approach would be: LOCAL MEMBER WASHED UP.

It's fun. It's now. It's entertainment. And it's so upfront to be downmarket. (ACP classed its rival, *Who Weekly*, as 'very upmarket', so you can imagine how far down downmarket is.) The bright ones can laugh at the jazziness, while the mugs can ponder the strange, incredible mysteries of the tunnel to Tibet under Ayers Rock. Down, ever down . . .

Why doesn't anyone buck the trend? Because we're all too busy making a buck, or trying to. It's worse since the fall of the Berlin Wall. Until then, the market-driven economies looked over their shoulders to sneer at the failures of communism, and it slowed us down. Now that the free market has triumphed, it's hell-for-leather and the logic of book-keeping is transformed into a social philosophy. In the death throes of Marxism, its perpetrator laughs from the inferno. As he foresaw, we are internalizing the values of the market-place, so nothing is either good or bad, but cash-flow makes it so. While the eighties are over, most of us confuse our self-worth with net worth.

It's old-fashioned and élitist to judge. Mickey Mouse is as mighty as Monet, Heavy Metal is as moving as Mozart. William Shawcross, the highbrow biographer of Rupert Murdoch, claims the British tabloid the *Sun* is his favourite newspaper, because of its sizzle and wit. At a media dinner party, when my wife lamented the salacious vulgarity of TV's *Hard Copy*, one of its producers fumed: 'Your type is content with the ABC test pattern.'

Just as the redneck politicians link the decline of beef sales to the rise of gay power, I have my own mad theories about the triumph of trash culture. It started with marijuana. The middle class found it was fun to get stoned and watch Joan Crawford movies. Then it was only a few short puffs to the ecstasies of *Dallas* and divining the riveting significance of ads for Pizza Hut. Along came the French, who can make 'pass the marmalade' sound like a new philosophy, and suddenly we have sub-texts, simulacra and the archaeology of the frivolous. Next, there'll be a master's degree on the *National Enquirer*'s homage to Gutenberg.

For intellectuals of another era, the very idea of evaluating newspapers is absurd. Their mere existence is a sign of social decay. Schopenhauer referred to journalists as 'little dogs', who barked at anything that moved. All are alarmists, he wrote, thinking of the *National Enquirer*, 'It's their way of making themselves interesting.' Chinese lawmakers foresaw the debilitating impact of media, even before it was invented. Statutes were aimed at keeping merchants – incipient press barons – separate from the rest of the community and blocking their social status. In the T'ang Dynasty, 'no merchant was permitted to ride on a horse or wear rich clothes'. That would have kept Murdoch out of our hair.

It's tragic that so few proprietors control so many publications. There's hardly room on the shelf for challenging
alternatives, much less the funds to kick them off.

An ancient Australian magazine had this maxim as its motto:
'One bright reader is worth a thousand boneheads.' These days
the reverse is the rule.

(*The Australian*)

Postscript

Happy to say, the experiment failed and the home-grown
Enquirer was confined to oblivion, along with the unclaimed
penis.

18
Off with the Pixies

Being on the road as an explorer for Extra Dimensions *put me through a lot of experiences that I would have preferred to read about in books. On camera, they looked silly or embarrassing – like the time I collapsed while taking a leak at a rebirthing session in Big Sur – but in the mind they added flashes of insight. Perhaps there is something at the core of the 'New Age' which is inimical to explication by the media. But that didn't stop me having a bash.*

1993:

The New Age is older than the book of Genesis and just as wise and full of baloney. Clay figures excavated from the Indus valley, dating from 3000 BC, show people in postures of yogic meditation. The first literary reference to the practice of yoga – the divine science of being and becoming – is found in the Vedas, the oldest books in the world. By comparison, the tale of Adam and Eve is a flash in the pan. For many, yoga is a doorway into the New Age. What starts off in a church hall as a stomach-flattening exercise can lead to intimations of divinity. But it's not the only doorway.

The New Age is today's brand name for a jumble of ideas, products and esoteric practices, ranging from the sublime to the shoddy, which Aldous Huxley dubbed 'the perennial philosophy'. In essence, it denotes a shift in the way we view the world and our place in it.

Although derided by the media, the precepts of the movement

percolate into popular culture: in hit movies (*Ghost, Dances with Wolves, The Doctor, The Fisher King*), in best-sellers (by Robert Bly, Shirley Maclaine, Ben Elton, Scott Peck), in TV Shows (from Oprah Winfrey to Joseph Campbell) and at the record stalls, with ambient sound, and the shopping malls, with float tanks, herbalists, crystals, naturopaths . . . The road less travelled is a gridlocked freeway.

According to Carl A. Raschke, a professor of religious studies, the New Age is 'the most powerful social force in the US today'. On the front page of the *New York Times*, he warned that it was as much a 'political movement as a religious movement' . . . and that it was infiltrating into all walks of life. 'If you look at it carefully you see it represents a complete rejection of Judeo-Christian beliefs and bedrock American values'. Perhaps this is no bad thing. The fact is, on its loopier side, the New Age bolsters American values, especially the bedrock value of shopping. Today's hot products include blown-glass wizards, feather-crystal amulets, polar power magnets, and chakra-tuned singing quartz crystal bowls.

As a label, the New Age is yukky; shunned by those who discreetly try to enrich their reverence for life, harness their potential and connect the crises facing the world with their personal habits. As with 'hippie' in the sixties, used more often by tabloids than the stoned revellers in the thick of a peace march, the label is aimed at marginalizing a movement which seems, on the face of it, incomprehensible, silly and – most of all – threatening.

While New Age can be compressed to rhyme with sewage, it can also, like the derided sludge, prove useful as compost. The core ideas are not original. Saints and philosophers have been burnt alive for espousing the credo, 'unity of all life' and the possibility of direct personal experience of God. William Blake said it forever – *to see the world in a grain of sand and heaven in a wild flower* – and John Donne added the politics – *one man's death diminishes all mankind.* In this century, Carl Jung shone a beam into the web of human connectedness, and unravelled archetypes of the collective unconscious. He foresaw the link between the decline of the sacred and the rise of the profane – a neat insight into today's disarray.

Countless others – deep ecologists, errant scientists, hands-on healers, futurists, entrepreneurs and 'barefooted economists' – have been beavering away at the boundaries of knowledge and wisdom.

So vast and vaporous is the drift of perennial philosophy into the mainstream, that it's like trying to describe the swirling of snow. In moments of self-importance, I have given speeches on the subject to corporate corrections, focusing on the three Cs – connectedness, compassion and consciousness.

The first C is obvious, and often repressed. We are all connected. Each of our actions or thoughts is linked to the global community and our own wellbeing. Individuals are not, as bemoaned by existentialists, shrunken and isolated, bobbing on a sea of ennui or despair, futile and forgotten. The choice of our morning drink, whether coffee or carrot juice, will impact on our metabolism, on the soil and probably on the economy of a distant land. Is the coffee a cash crop, grown on a plantation at the behest of the World Bank? Is it impoverishing the villagers, by denying them acreage to cultivate their own gardens, or impoverishing the soil, by draining its nutrients, or impoverishing the economy, by making it overly dependent on commodity prices?

Posing such questions for many years is Bill Mollison, the creator of Permaculture – the perennial agriculture – a philosophy of gardening and land management which defies the industrial model. It aims to place all the elements of a living system in the right relationship to each other; a Feng Shui of soil and soul. If Mollison had his way, I suspect, all our front lawns would be market gardens and our pet dogs would be ground into compost. The change in his media image, incidentally, from weirdo to eco guru, is a process likely to be repeated again and again, as news-managers wake up to the issues that have long been the staple of fringe magazines.

Making connections goes beyond politics and economics. The Rainforest Action Network plays its part in political lobbying, but its real battleground is the psyche. John Seed's Council of All Beings (COABS) are convened all over the world, often in partnership with therapists and ecologists. COABS are rituals set in the outdoors, which forge a dramatic visceral connection between human participants and entities from other realms, be they animal, vegetable or mineral. Involving psychodrama, visualizations, rolling in mud, confessions and reversals, the COABS trigger a psycho-spiritual journey into the viewpoint of non-humans – a journey that has a lingering, even lifelong impact on those involved. (It's not as mad as it seems: Hokusai – *If you want to draw a bird, you must become a bird.*)

John Seed's own revelation occurred at a confrontation with bulldozers, when he 'realized' he was not just a radical defending the rainforest, but that he was, in some strange way, an extension of the forest defending itself.

In the field of medicine, the connection has firmed between body and mind, leading to the stratospheric rise of holistic health, the 'third revolution' in Western medicine, after surgery and penicillin.

The second C, compassion, also flies in the face of the post-modernist penchant for irony and detachment, and evokes memories of the Good Samaritan, that Biblical wimp. With the decline of guru-mania and the rise of AIDS, people have been forced to combine their yen for holiness with hands-on fieldwork. The buzzword is service.

The self-help therapy groups and support networks for AIDS sufferers are legendary, prompting endorsements from unlikely sources. 'And yet what I saw was deeply impressive,' writes Charles Moore in the *Spectator* (7 May 1988). 'The generation of West Coast Americans who talked inanely and incessantly

about Love in the sixties and seventies are now being asked to
love in harsh circumstances and they are responding. Many on
the Shanti Project show the unconditional love which is the
highest thing demanded by religion.'

In the early seventies, the protest generation suffered a
three-way tug between lefty politics, stalking their bliss and
building their bank balance. A pivotal book at the time was
Be Here Now, by Baba Ram Dass, a former colleague of
Timothy Leary at Harvard. His purple paperback was funny
and intriguing, sharpening Western desire for a grab-bag of
Eastern doctrines aiming at the elimination of desire. An
obscure guru was featured, mistily photographed, who was
said to be so spaced-out that when he was fed handfuls of LSD
by his acolytes, he shrugged and continued drinking his tea.

Twenty years later, Ram Dass is still on the lecture circuit.
LSD has been replaced with the concept of 'service' – good
works performed in direct contact with the recipients; whether
it's sending goats to Guatemala or treating glaucoma in Nepal.
'In the sixties I learnt how to *be*, but not how to *do*,' he says,
noting that his focus is on Karma yoga – using service to others
as a path to transformation.

Known as 'the new altruism', this trend has a slogan: *doing
good is good for you*. After decades of working with the
sick and the dying, Ram Dass glows with good health; a
phenomenon backed by the latest research, which shows
that altruism boosts the immune system. Dr Dean Ornish
is so convinced of the healing power of compassion that he
sometimes forces bickering patients in his therapy group to
do each other's laundry. 'Such selfless acts,' he says, 'reduce
cholesterol level and chest pains.'

We can all acquire this immunity shield, it's a relief to learn,
without actually doing good ourselves. It's sufficient to watch
other people doing good. Students who were shown films of
Mother Theresa in Calcutta, while hooked up to diagnostic
computers, registered a rise in immunity levels.

Compassion is a key because it dictates the politics of the future. How can you fight to save an obscure tree kangaroo if you don't care a hoot about animals? Statistics alone do not enlarge the heart, but meditation might. Imagine a slow, trance-like ritual, where each individual in a roomful of strangers is asked to contemplate the person they most love. 'Stay with this feeling,' asks the facilitator, 'nourish this feeling and then let it envelop the next layer of people you care about' . . . and then the next, and the next, and so on, until the original emotion extends beyond your intimates to reach the neighbourhood, community, village, city, country, religion, nation, globe, so that when the lights flick on and you open your eyes, the strangers in the room shimmer beside you like long-lost friends. Surely this is a force more powerful than politics, and yet it is politics.

Realists may snort at the 'compassion industry' and TV commentators deride the 'touchy-feelie' waffle of New Agers, but practical compassion is a trend which is tickling the cash register. 'Doing good is no longer an option,' writes Faith Popcorn, the indomitable consultant to American Express, Citibank and Coca-Cola, 'doing good is a must.' She cites a course offered by Cornell University's School of Hotel Administration – 'Housing and Feeding the Homeless'.

The third C is consciousness. Can it be raised? How high? What the hell?

In Homer's day, soldiers prayed for cosmic consciousness, or Menos, 'the state of mental intoxication induced in humans by Gods or other supernatural agencies' (James Lasdun). It frequently descended on the eve of battle. Menos is 'moral spunk' – a rush of fortitude, derring-do and wisdom. In the thick of today's environmental battle, Menos is what people are praying for now. It's a tricky area.

In the sixties, babyboomers came to see that consciousness was malleable, after they had soaked it in LSD – Woweeaaiigh!!??! KABOOM!! – and that it was also fragile.

Then came the consoling years of meditation, yoga and fasting, when people thought nirvana was just around the corner, or at least in Uttar Pradesh. Meanwhile, a few Western psychologists were shifting focus from pathology to the study of optimal mental states. (It was noted that Freud's works contained over 400 references to neurosis and none to health.) Abraham Maslow charted the hierarchies of human needs, maintaining that once the necessities of life were met, 'self-actualization' became a primary goal.

Drawing on the grass roots popularism of the Power of Positive Thinking, and combining it with insights from the Eastern mystical tradition, a new confidence was invested in humans to solve their own problems. Dubbed the Human Potential Movement, this precursor of the New Age was dismissed as a solipsistic fad of the Me Generation; indulgent and silly. People bounding out of hot tubs at Big Sur after their Primal Screams, asking the eternal question – anyone for the inner game of tennis?

A generation shifted its attention from matter to mind. A seventies handbook was *How to Get High Without Drugs*, and psychologists began to map the peaks and plateaux of altered states. There were six realms of existence, according to Tibetans, while John Lilly, stoned at the centre of the cyclone, nominated twelve. Sanskrit boasted over twenty words to designate distinct levels of awareness.

It is now argued that the clarity of perception, sense of identity, muscular response, range of emotions and luminosity of thought, are all functions which vary with states of consciousness. To sharpen these functions, teachers routinely draw on an array of mystical techniques. A phrase from today's locker rooms is 'playing in the zone', and even the Green Berets have been taught how to meditate.

Once associated with 'going nuts', the quest for transcendence has come to be seen as a therapeutic end in itself.

But how does this help the rest of the world? Basically,

because our continued existence of us as a species is threatened by the curse of human pathology, the limitation of our mental make-up. In the past we have been able to act out our immaturities rather than having to understand them or outgrow them, 'to indulge our addictions rather than resolve them, and to revolve through the same neurotic patterns rather than evolve out of them' (Roger Walsh, *Revision*, 1985). Creatures of habit, we need to change faster than a speeding bullet, to become superhuman, or at least, super-sensitive humans. And nothing changes behaviour quicker than a leap of awareness.

Nine years ago, while driving through Rajasthan, in northern India, I noticed the windswept desert was dotted with patches of green. These settlements – thick with woodlands and wild life – belong to the Bishnoi, a half-million tribe of farmers (see page 47), whose prosperity, the envy of the state, is linked with a vision – life is only worth living if you let others live – and this includes animals, birds and insects.

In January 1990, Joel Rubin, a seventeen-year-old high school student from Maine, saw footage on TV of dolphins being slaughtered in tuna nets, and was astounded that 'humans could murder them so brutally'. Rubin felt that if his parents had seen the same program, they would have commented 'that's too bad about dolphins, but that's life'. He rooted out the home addresses of three executives at HJ Heinz, the parent company of StarKist, the world's largest producer of tinned tuna. He sent them letters of protest, which were ignored. Rubin roped in seventy-five students to pound the executives with postcards.

At a press conference that April, the managing director of Heinz unexpectedly announced that his company would no longer market tuna caught at the expense of dolphins, and he quoted a line from a student's card: 'How can you sleep at night knowing your company is doing this?'

Easy, unfortunately, for most magnates. Which is why spiritual practices are important – to help us progress from self-centredness to reality-centredness. If a flash of insight can green the desert or save the dolphin, maybe a collective vision can change the world.

(*HQ Magazine*)

At the Council of All Beings

'Go off into the forest and get into a calm, meditative state,' he said. 'Try and identify with another being – a non-human being. It could be a bird, an animal, an insect or even an element . . . like the wind.' It was a cloudy Sunday in March, and a dozen or so people leant against eucalypts or sat on logs, listening to John Seed, convenor of the Council. 'When you return,' he continued, 'we will ask you to make a mask of the being you've chosen to represent – or maybe they've chosen to represent you – and to speak for that being at the Council of All Beings.' My field notes:

With masks attached, we sit in a circle for a long time, saying nothing. The effect is impressive. A tiger, a fly, a kookaburra, a tree-fern, an ant . . . a fairytale world of other beings sit opposite me. Gone are the humans, and with them my internal repertoire of critical responses. The atmosphere is church-like.

'I speak today on behalf of the rainforests of the world,' says a voice from behind a delicate shield of twigs and leaves, 'and of all the species of plants and animals that I contain.' This plea comes from John Seed, an eco-activist who has helped create this ritual involving theatre and therapy in order to de-programme our 'human chauvinism' – the belief that humans are the crown of creation and the source of all value. Humans are but one strand in the fabric of life, he argues, they did not create life. Nor was life created for their benefit.

To some extent, all species are chauvinists, as Wendell Berry has pointed out: 'An earthworm, I think, is living in an earthworm-centred world; the thrush who eats the earthworm is living in a thrush-centred world; the hawk who eats the thrush . . .' But none of these creatures is equipped with the same powers of disruption and dominance that humans have – humans would happily exterminate earthworm, thrush, hawk and many others if it meant a better breakfast cereal.

Part of our being here, I suppose, is to purge our minds of Genesis: 'and upon every fowl of the air, and upon all that moveth on the earth, and upon all the fishes of the sea; into your hands they are delivered.'

John Seed believes that when we peel back our layers of 'anthropocentric cherishing' and spend time in the forest surrendering to its myriad complexity, its intelligence and its 135 million years of history, then something extraordinary happens. Our emotions, our values – our being . . . is transformed. We *become* the rainforest. It's not an intellectual identification, but a sudden, striking, spiritual conversion.

'You humans evolved for hundreds of millions of years in my moist, green womb,' continues the rainforest, 'before emerging a scant five million years ago, blinking into the light.'

John Seed's own conversion happened in the forest, amidst danger. A one-time IBM executive, his 'ecological self' awoke when he put his body between the wilderness and advancing chainsaws. As with many other activists, the initial stance of 'I am protecting the rainforest,' soon evolved into 'I am the rainforest protecting myself,' and then further, into 'I am that part of the rainforest which has recently emerged into thinking.'

But what kind of thinking? Is it really possible to be a rainforest? To think like a rainforest? There is certainly something about Seed's voice which *sounds* like a rainforest.

'I wish to speak with alarm about what is happening to the skies . . . the fierce rays are sapping my strength.'

Much to my own surprise, I take up the pause: 'Forgive me, Rainforest. The protective membrane between us is being torn apart. I am the light, the power, the giver of life. Now things are out of balance and I can't control my own strength. Please, Earth, don't make me lose control.'

As I stop, with an unexpected lump in my throat, there is a reassuring chorus from the group: 'We hear you, Sun!'

'I speak for the tree-fern,' says a gentle female, 'please wake up to how delicate the balance in the bush is. My life depends on many other species, just as their life depends on me.'

'I speak for all the insects – the dragonfly, the sandfly and even the humble housefly – we have our place, too. You don't have to kill us – just flick us away. When you spray us with insecticides, you poison the earth. So by killing us you are killing yourselves.'

'I am the being within the rock,' intones an appropriately husky German accent, 'not yet formed. I view with amused detachment the ways of people. If they annihilate themselves, that doesn't matter very much . . . but if they annihilate the earth, that's a problem, because from deep inside of me, new life can come.'

As each being speaks, the mood becomes increasingly sombre. The voices discard their human identities. She who speaks for the kookaburra is no longer 'an architect'; the wind is no longer 'a model'. Everyday assumptions seem to change. No one questions the right of the rock to have feelings. Gone is that seemingly crucial distinction between 'life' and 'lifeless'.

John Seed believes that as the implications of ecology and evolution are internalized, our atavistic memory improves. First, there is an identification with all life, and then with the inorganic material from which life has sprung. 'Remember our childhood as minerals?' he asks. 'As lava, as rocks?'

'I speak for the kingdom of Ant. I am a bit upset. Why are

you all so serious? I am more simple, working all day. What's
the problem about dying? I live off destruction. I'm happy with
it. As an ant, I'm quite busy. This planet is a big playground.
We all have to die. Take it easy. Stop complaining.'

'That's all very well for you, Ant. You live underground, but
us tigers of Bengal, we live in the jungle . . . and it's disappearing.
Before, humans never used to come near us, but now they're all
over the place. Just the other day, my best friend was killed by
a human – just because he had eaten one of them. What else
could he do? There isn't any game anymore.'

When all the beings had spoken, Seed called for a volunteer;
someone to take off their mask and sit inside the circle, to be
human and answer the criticisms. No one stirred.

I was a bit sick of my mask. It wasn't as elegant as the rest –
the string was broken and I was tired of holding the cardboard
over my face, squinting through slits. Anyway, it was time to
remind these normally speechless entities about Shakespeare
and Notre Dame. So I sat in the middle of the circle, and was
immediately sorry. It was like being in a dock, with the accusers
angelic, gifted, deeply wronged and yet forgiving. What's more,
I actually felt guilty. Have *you* ever tried to take on the crimes
of humanity – not the ones against each other, but the ones
committed against everything else? It's crushing.

'And you're always so depressed,' the ant droned on, 'even
with all your wantonness and power.'

'But humans do try to have fun with chainsaws and four-
wheel drives,' moaned another, 'so expensive and damaging.'

'It was fatal to let you think you have dominion over us,'
said the dolphin. 'It just turned you into efficient killers.'

'And all that anger inside you,' said a serene lioness, 'you
just take out on us.'

And so on. Fortunately, the rainforest intervened. 'It's a pretty
sad human,' he said. 'But I do believe that among your species
there are some who do wish to represent our interests. Before

closing this Council of All Beings, I'd like us to consider what sort of gifts we can offer these humans who wish to work on our behalf – what kind of powers can we give them?

'You're going to need tenacity,' he continued, 'because you don't yet realize the enormity of the changes ahead. As a rainforest which has existed for millions of years, I give you tenacity.'

'We tigers would like to offer you our example of loving ourselves. We're beautiful and great. We can walk proudly and fear no one. We offer you courage.'

'Spirit of wind would like to offer you power – it's free. If you were to use me, which you may do at any time, you need not destroy the earth. I also offer you my playfulness . . .'

As the sun set, the Council of All Beings drew to a close. After thanking their adopted beings, everyone threw their masks into the fire, so releasing the spirits into the air.

For the rest of the weekend, few of us could walk along a trail without worrying about the insects we crushed. Some went as far as to 'make a deal' with the mosquitoes: 'You may suck my blood with impunity,' they would say aloud to them, 'as long as you keep away from my face.'

19
Yum Yum Tom Yum

*The triumph of multiculturalism in Australia, the
economic rise of the Asian Tigers and the psychic
drift towards becoming a Republic have focused
attention on our neighbours in the 'far' East. But
what about the inner West?*

1993:

By the third spoonful of Tom Yum soup, the sweat streamed
down my dial, just like it should. The kids suspiciously sipped
their health juice – a blend of lime rind, ginseng and durian. On
the footpath, Vietnamese hoods hustled their contraband of
pirated Microsoft. At last – the real Asia! Caucasians were rare.
Outside the Chinese herbalist's, the shoppers jostled in throngs
for the special-of-the-day – powdered shark fins. Where was I?
Not in a remote province of Szechuan, but at a multi-cultural
shopping mall in the Western suburbs . . . of Sydney.

Cabramatta – pearl of the Orient. The Hong Kong of the
Hume Highway; the Far East of the Inner West.

Yum Yum Tom Yum. Pass the fire bucket. Being here is more
fun than being there. And it's cheaper. No planes, no bookings,
no touristy hordes clutching their Lonely Planet Guides, no
pimps, cops, creepie-crawlies, coup d'états . . . Do I sound
like a cowardly fusspot? I've spent half my life drifting across
Asia, picking up cheap thrills and costly diseases. You lot were
still in your playpen while I was slurping Mai Tai cocktails in
a bamboo shack in a transit lounge on the edge of a swamp;
now known as Singapore Airport.

Yup; I was a pot-head in Cambodia before Pol Pot, and a

backpacker in Patpong before ping-pong. Don't talk to me about the Exotic East. It was all over the minute they installed air-conditioning. Our Cabramatta is more authentic than Kuala Lumpur, more mysterious than the Mekong Delta. Crates of unknown sea species are stacked at the fish market, flipping and flapping; the strangest greens tumble into the aisle.

Sadly, last Saturday, I saw an ominous shift in the prevailing race mix. In addition to the faint sprinkle of peace-worker types and elderly missionaries, a busload of well-heeled Caucasian shoppers alighted at Chieng Mai Bridalwear. Then they were herded through the supermarket by an Indian woman in baggy jeans and a hand-mike, who explained the purpose of inscrutable foodstuffs – cassava crackers from Indonesia; pickled okra from Orissa, bats' beaks from Burma. It was the official *Women's Weekly* tour of the exotic West.

Oh well, why not? We all learn from each other. The hand that rocks the wok rules the future. I relocate to a kerbside tea stall, savouring fine French percolated coffee, as a Vietnamese hood tries to panhandle the gamelan buskers. At the next table, two elderly men with white goatees, both looking like Lao Tse, play mah-jong. A sign outside the dreary estate agent's shop-front proclaims: 'We speak Mandarin, Lao, Thai, Burmese, Cantonese, Khmer, Malay, Hindi and English.' Pretty soon, I am thinking, on foreign shores they'll be offering tourist packages to this neck of the Orient.

An old song drifts from the mists of nostalgia: Cabramatta heeere I cooome/ right back where I started frooom . . .

Just then, a young woman clutching a clipboard makes an approach. 'We're doing a doco about this fabulous place. Care to be interviewed?' No thanks. Maybe if I shut my big mouth for a change, this joint might hang on a bit longer. It's like I'm back in the bar on the edge of a Singapore swamp, just as the jack-hammers begin blasting away.

(*Asian Business Review*)

20
A Mug, a Radio, a Woollen Singlet

Protest and dropping out was one way of attack-
ing the 'dominant paradigm', and so was buil-
ding alternative communities. Another way is to
re-invent capitalism. Over the years, I became
intrigued by the idealism of the 'barefoot econo-
mists' such as Paul Hawken, Guy Dauncey and
Hazel Henderson, who prod corporations to shift
from being part of the problem to becoming part
of the solution. When I was invited to address
corporate conventions on social issues, I endorsed
the trend of social responsibility, or 'capitalism
with a conscience'. This led to a regular column
in the Australian Business Monthly *(ABM) – now*
extinct, doubtless because they failed to implement
my new economic agenda.

1993:

Corporations cross national borders with ease, but can they
transcend the borders of their own imagination? This is
the decade of tumult and transformation. Artists obliterate
boundaries; ecologists glorify inter-dependence. It's a time for
capitalists to come in from the cold.

In previous eras of social upheaval, the corporation was seen
as the enemy. (Down with Dow Chemicals!) How boring it
was in the sixties and seventies for executives to watch from
the office window in their white shirts while the longhairs
marched against the war, chanted Dylan and celebrated free
love. Actually, not so boring if your product was right: flared

jeans, frisbees and love beads. Product and protest go hand in hand in the West, where the commodification of dissent is a lifestyle.

Millionaire Michael Jackson makes video clips which resonate with menace and system-wrecking. Spike Lee's movies celebrate the Outsider and blast bourgeois morality, as does the director in person, who can be seen regularly on US prime time, promoting the world's most expensive athletic shoe. Local cleanskin Johnny Farnham is shown on Ampol billboards with a motorbike and a Driz-a-bone, instilling a warm glow into ageing rockers and extolling a deep love for the Sunburnt Country. In real life, in small print, we read that Ampol petroleum has been fined $30,000 for fouling the waterways.

In the future, the ad agencies may not so easily buy off dissent. The corporation will need to reinvent itself, enlarging its role and horizon. Just like the guard at the NSW Art Gallery, Derek Barson, who enclosed himself in a plastic cube, in which he sat on a stool in uniform, raising PhD conundrums about his old role and turning himself into a performance artist. Apple Corp is renowned for its aspiration to empower people through the use of personal computers and 'to make the world a better place'. If that sounds soppy, you're stuck in the past.

OK, so it's a recession. Economists from Adam Smith to Milton Friedman have argued that national prosperity is best assured by the pursuit of profit alone, leaving social benefits to accrue with the nudge of an 'invisible hand'. Uh huh. Open slather is no longer feasible in a world of depleted resources, social decay and global trauma. The wealth of nations is secondary to the health of nations; which is why 'barefooted economists' have devised alternative indicators to the GNP. Hazel Henderson, a futurist consulted by the Fortune 500 and a contributor to the *Harvard Business Review*, proposes the Country Futures Indicators (CFI), which collates data on education, literacy, health care, life expectancy, and political participation. To which

I would add soil degradation, public space, volunteerism and laughter.

The US scores abysmally on voter participation, literacy and health care, whereas Kerala, in India, with one of the lowest per capita incomes in the world, has a 'very high quality of life', as reflected in the CFI. This may plummet when the inhabitants are given Hondas and told to run advertising agencies, as in Delhi.

In the West, future consumers will move beyond the cycle of adorning themselves with rebellious images and rap haircuts, to become part of a process of shopping and investing in a critical manner. The sharp consumer will demand that prices include social and environmental costs. (Noise, dirty water, its destiny as landfill.) Wasteful products will become unaffordable and unfashionable. The clever company will put enriching the community before enriching its senior executives.

Enlightened entrepreneurs are the revolutionaries of the future, using the might of money to instigate a shift in priorities, instead of invoking the image of leathery rebels to create an illusion of reform. That truculent pin-up in *Rolling Stone* has no intention of storming the Bastille – he's desperate for a brand of blue suede shoes to endorse. 'Rebel' today is a buzzword, as T. C. Frank points out, meaning 'I'm sexy and unreliable, and I want your money.'

Who am I to talk, being both victim and a promoter of the rhetoric of radicalism, probably derived from too much James Dean at an early age? We pooh-poohed the values of our forebears, who avoided restaurants, saved string, wore cardigans, declined credit and didn't buy what they didn't need, or even what they did. After the death of my father, who was a devoted, slogging, successful company chairman, I found that his personal belongings fitted into an overnight bag – a coffee mug, a cheap radio, a woollen singlet, a captured Japanese flag, bits and pieces. Yet I was the one who spouted on about the evils of consumerism, in between buying LPs or floral shirts, while he merely refused to consume. Maybe the shoppers of the future are more like my father – give or take a computer or two – than Spike Lee, Michael Jackson or me.

(*Australian Business Monthly*)

21
Zen Master Neil Armstrong

Those who most loudly bemoan the effects of the sixties often hark back to a golden age of untrammelled progress and do-as-thou-wilt capitalism – the fifties. My generation may have been narcissistic and spoilt, but what we wrecked most was ourselves. Another breed is targeting the whole world.

1993:

On a balmy Monday in February, the two men from Asia dropped out of the sky to a helipad in the Blue Mountains, and came by for afternoon tea. Measuring the vista with their eyes, they marvelled at the reddening cliffs, and contemplated building a tourist resort. 'Leave this town alone,' I said, passing the carrot cake, 'you've already rooted Bangkok.' They laughed – yes, Bangkok was a bit of a fuck-up – but that was the way of the world.

American Kit and Hong Kong Ken were gung-ho developers whose tentacles encircled the region. They had arrived in Sydney the previous day, *en route* to South Australia, where they had paid to be lowered under the ocean in cages to feed the sharks. 'You won't need the cages,' I said, 'it's the sharks I'm worried about.' Having met Kit in Asia fifteen years ago, making his first millions by franchising a pizza chain in Thailand, I knew the kind of damage he could inflict.

'You Aussies are a lazy lot,' he said, echoing the chorus of our Asian neighbours, striking at the heart of our destiny. More and more we are under attack . . . in word and deed. Whether it's editorials in a Singapore newspaper warning us to smarten up, or the table of Koreans at a local Japanese restaurant in Katoomba, who scream at the waitress for mishandling the napkins.

The attacks by a Japanese spokesman, Shuji Tomikawa, on contemporary America are worth pondering. 'The US had once been a great place but threw it away with the liberalism of the 1960s' (*Pacific Rift* by Michael Lewis). While it was 'great for the individual', it was also . . . 'a disaster'. This is the view of a lot of Japanese, apparently, who believe the West should 'rewind its body clocks to 1950'. (It would then be in sync with Kit and Ken's, who are now planning shopping malls in Rangoon.) According to Mr Tomikawa, 'Sixties parents will regret their entire lives when they die.' Oh dear.

So there you have it, finally, some frank talk from Japan. The whole debate in a nutshell. Is that applause I hear from our entrepreneurs? If we want to shine in the Asian bloc, then it's roll up the sleeves, turn back the clock, unleash the bulldozers. What a load of crap.

We'd be dead in no time. Why salivate over the achievements of Japan, when the country is a nutcase; in deep, neurotic denial over the environmental impact of its greed? Whether it's slaughtering sea creatures, felling the forests or fouling the ozone, the Japanese are so busy prostrating themselves at the altar of Progress that they haven't noticed the fragility of the future. Their 'three sacred treasures' of the nineties are a car, a colour TV and air-conditioning. So far from regretting their lives on their deathbeds, the sixties pioneers will bemoan the rise of Japan.

And as for the admonishments of Singapore – the sterile conformity of that unfree island is not one Australia needs emulate. Sure, Kit and Ken are having a ball as they build the new Asia (one is providing the air-conditioning for the other's new mall and they plan to seal the deal, appropriately, in the shark cage). While these two developers know in their bones their projects are killing the quality of life, they don't know any other way to live. Which is where Australia comes in – not with the fake borrowed lifestyle of fancy hotels, stretch limos and millionaire stunts, but in a quietly emerging alternative Oz, focusing on simple pleasures, vast virgin beauty, sustainable livelihood and a slower pace (tranquillity is a resource, you idiot critics, not something of which to be ashamed).

One day it will dawn on those with the vaunted fifties 'body-clocks' that lifestyle is something to be experienced, not an artefact to be marketed.

Those who years ago cut themselves adrift from rat-race city centres are re-emerging with processes and products grown organically from their own experience; ones unique and in high demand. 'Adding value' before it became a buzzword. Meditation tapes and surfing gear, honey from an ancient breed of Ligurian bees and eucalyptus oils from Kangaroo Island, Bliss Shoes, blown glass and Sanctuary skin care from Byron Bay . . . plus countless items which stimulate the local economy and psychology, without costing the earth.

Ours is a land of infinite secrets . . . and undervalued resources. It is so foolish to try to make Oz conform to an image from afar. The mass media treat us as an 'economy', first and foremost, whereas all of us actually live in a society. Real wealth is a mixture of material potential, environmental health and cultural diversity – habits, values, interests, street gear, cuisine, manners, sexual behaviour, sunsets, night sky, education, religion, architecture, beaches, philosophy, crafts, arts, colours, rituals, music, dancing, mythology, dreams . . .

It is the Asians within Australia that are adding value, rather than the ones outside, and not only in the obvious way, which is gastronomically. At a nearby mountain meditation retreat for ten days (too long for me) a friend was surprised at the proportion of Asian immigrants joining the fast-growing band of Aussies 'entering the stream' of enlightenment seekers. There, he met a Cambodian boy with the unlikely name of Neil

Armstrong. After landing in Sydney, the Cambodian had flicked through a book on heroes of space, and was so taken with the famous name that he adopted it as his own. Neil endeared himself to his fellow meditators by cleaning out the toilet block single-handed.

When I get mad at Shuji Tomikawa for his harking back to the fifties, extolling consumption and conformity, I think of Neil Armstrong, the new arrival with a generous soul, a practical streak and cosmic aspirations, the boy with a rag-mop, a sprig of gumleaf in his hair . . . and reaching for the moon.

(*ABM*)

22
Grey Flannel Scum Marketing

As someone who helped popularize the concept of Youth Culture, I deserve to be shocked by the way advertisers hurl themselves at the feet of the baby busters.

1993:

Trends are the foreplay of the Future, making marketers salivate. But what if it's a tease? All dazzle, no delivery. Collapsed hopes, wet pants, rising anger. Beware the trend teasers. The most fertile field for this faddish game – itself a trend – is youth. What's happening? The great marketing dream is to understand and map a huge cult of conformist youth with its own music, fabric, fast food, shoes, software and holiday resorts. The brood of the baby boomers.

No one has quite coined a term, but the race is on. First there was the wry, flat, ironic novel by Douglas Copeland, *Generation X*, with its landscape of dead end McJobs, mid-twenties breakdowns, throwaway Swedish furniture and legislated nostalgia (the forcing of youth to have memories they don't possess, like Woodstock or Camelot). 'Look out yuppie scum,' warns the cover quote, 'here come the Xers'.

The fun lies in the margin notes, invented by an editor, with their pithy putdowns: 'Bleeding ponytail – an elderly sold-out baby boomer who pines for hippie or pre-sellout days.' Xers are supposedly a lost generation of bicycle couriers and office temps from split families, scarred by recession and the collapse of Greed, prone to Boomer Envy and jetflights to nowhere, with a life-view moulded by "Elvis Moments", sitcoms and knee-jerk irony. Most of all, they are "fiercely suspicious of being lumped together as an advertiser's target market". But that doesn't stop the trend teasers.

The US mag *Business Week* devoted a special issue to Generation X, involving five reporters, 'bureau feeds', stat charts, marketing hype and flim-flam headlines: Move Over, Boomers . . . here come The Busters . . . 46 million people between eighteen and twenty-nine . . . coming on strong . . . about to change our lives. Yes, but who are they? The senior vice-president for marketing at Taco Bell Worldwide is hailed for his in-depth research into this mysterious, elusive offspring of the Pepsi Generation. His discovery? 'They love music, they love to party, and they love irreverence.' Blow me down. So that's a million dollar marketing insight? Find me a twentysomething generation that doesn't like to party and I'll find you a Shopping Mall with soul.

The overall Xer attitude, according to the cover story, is 'grunge, anger, cultural dislocation, a secret yearning to belong'. For those of you who haven't lately travelled on suburban trains, grunge is an ill-kempt, daggy, shirt-tail flapping, untied sneaker look, which saves on laundry. Replace grunge with jazz, and you have the leotards scene of the fifties; the Beat Generation. Replace grunge with pot and we jump to the anti-war anger and cultural dislocation of the next decade.

In its eagerness to transform the novel into a youthquake, *Business Week* copped a tidal wave of protest. 'Seven pages of grey flannel scum marketing bullshit,' opined one youngster in a New York give-way tabloid, who dismissed all youth marketing as 'Fun, challenging, but a crapshoot'. At best, the survey was likened to Polaroid Scholarship, fuzzy, unreal, lacking depth. One critic conceded there 'might be a few whiny snots out there who vaguely conform to the profile', just as 'there were a few beatniks who really did wear goatees and berets and say "go cat, go"', but this fanciful hepcat was no less a creation of a 'hostile and clueless media' than the concocted Generation X.

All in all, a bogus trend. The real leaders of the new generation are still underground, insists a hopeful Boomer, 'tinkering with Virtual Reality, Environmental Science, interactive video and the like . . . These clues have probably sparked a frenzy of undercover surveillance by marketing wizards, keen to supplant Generation X, the Beat-en Generation, with a more romantic and cinematic style of adolescent . . . Captain Video meets the Rainbow Warrior. Welcome to a new market, one yearning for computerized whitegoods, erotic software, organic silk suits, inflatable hemp sneakers and a post-New-Age theme park on the Gold Coast.

Meanwhile, the problems of teenage poverty, violence and dislocation don't seem to disappear with each new craze. The 'troublesome kids' themselves are often the repository of eloquence and wisdom. A gang member was asked by the ABC's *7.30 Report* why he so often bloodied his knuckles. 'Fighting makes me feel proud,' he said. 'It's the only thing I've got. In a few more years I'll be mowing lawns and cleaning lavatories for the rich.' Yeah. Right on, as we used to say. One sound-byte is worth a thousand sociology texts. These days, where can youth derive a sense of self-esteem, without reverting to the ape-like antics of the cave? (This is not only a recession, a friend remarked, it's a regression.)

If just a fraction of the energy put into selling to youth could be switched to working with youth, helping them hone a role for themselves in the new world order, then we could convert a heartache into a high goal. A few noble souls are trying, usually linked to churches or charities, but business is still locked in a Darwinian freeze-frame. Wake up. The world does not need another golf course, a gold-plated loo or five-star hotel. It needs a complete revolution of corporate culture, a re-statement of methods and goals which underlie all activity, including market research; a realization that the pursuit of profit alone, without hands-on social responsibility, is a profit for no one . . . in the end. To sell to the community, without helping to restore that community, is to sell the community short.

Shareholders can trade a few percentage points in return for going to sleep at night without locking their doors. Wouldn't you?

(ABM)

Turn on TV, Turn 23 off the World

Never mind the research. I would not have credited the effect of TV on human behaviour without seeing it at home first-hand. Finally, we locked the set in the cupboard, though suspicions had long been aroused.

1994:

Fast cars, fast images, fast travel, fast food; the mesh of modern life is hard to resist. Each strand supports the other. The crisp take-away chook wings that we munch watching TV are promoted as 'full of golden goodness' as it dribbles down our chin; a psychic feedback loop which becomes ever more encompassing. Just as we confuse TV with reality, we mistake ads for information. In real life, the chooks are immobilized, imprisoned, injected, dejected and deformed. Apart from questions of ethics and cruelty, there are human health risks. This is an alternative view, complicated and difficult to unearth, rarely put to air. These days, knowledge is market-driven.

A TV game show, *Videot*, demands of its bright young players an encyclopaedic knowledge of trivia and trash, thereby enhancing the importance of its own medium and reordering the priorities of youthful curiosity. No prizes if you don't recall the theme song of last year's hit soapie. Another new show, significantly sited on the cusp of the national news, reinforces the notion of Television as the Academy of Tomorrow. Let's hear it for Fred Flintstone's birthday . . .

Manufactured images, deep trivia and pseudo-information

('golden goodness') is starting to replace real life. Cairns is the focus of the great Oz tourist bonanza, an area, ssshhhh, that is wet for much of the year. The tourist intake is comprised of Japanese herds with thick wallets who are bussed from the airport to a luxury motor launch, where they are whisked off to inspect endangered coral in murky waters. But by the time they get to the reef, which they can't see, they have already viewed it. Shipboard video screens are loaded with a looped tape of Coral Dreams.

We are not equipped by evolution to distinguish in our minds between natural images and those which are artificially created and implanted – hence the implacable success of TV, and the triumph of the illusion. The mesh of the false is forever tightening. On the Daikyo reef cruise, not even the money is real. In order to shop, the passengers are compelled to exchange their dollars for 'cruise money', which heightens the illusion of foreign adventure and boosts the coffers (too boring to queue to change back). In this fast-growing industry, with the media at its feet, expressions of protest are met with a deaf ear. Let's not rock the cruise boat . . . In the resort hotels, the tourist TV channel is never off the air. It is always sunny.

At last, at last, there is a revival of protest against the feedback of falsehood. It is called Culture Jamming. This is a way of subverting, distorting or turning back on itself the message of mainstream media. The movement has its own heroes, T-shirts, anti-ads and – in Canada – a lively magazine and a lobby group. 'We will culture-jam the pop culture marketeers,' thunders the manifesto, 'On the rubble of the old media culture, we will build a new one with a non-commercial heart and soul.'

Culture Jamming can also involve deep and meaningful courses at universities and Zen-like experiments in the silence of one's living-room. A Canadian academic, Bernard McGrane, believes that every time we turn the TV on, we turn the world off. We are fooled into thinking we are watching things life-sized. To crack this illusion, and to make us aware that watching TV is actually a practice, an ongoing, persevering, and exhausting self-hallucination, he has devised several exercises. One of these is a TET or a Technical Events Test. A video camera attached to a traffic light or a bank ceiling just recording the passing scene. It is 'pure TV'. Anything else is a technical event: zooms, cutaways, close-ups, sound overlays, edits, fades, etc. For ten minutes, watch the news and count the technical events.

(His students get furious when asked to do this or other experiments, like watching without the sound, because it shifts the focus from set to self.) But counting the technical events brings about a paradigm shift. 'We are shocked into seeing what it is we've been doing all these years.' You see all the levers behind the illusion and realize how hard you've been working to weave the bits together in a coherent narrative. You've been in high gear without knowing it, an unconscious participant in a prison of make-believe. Now you see clearly, in McGrane's view, that TV is (1) training you to shorten your attention span, (2) making ordinary life seem dull, (3) injecting a hypnotic quality in your ordinary awareness and (4) coercing you into its reality; a consensus trance invoked by the camera, leaving us lifeless and unresisting.

Culture Jamming is about creating alternative realities. One group issues colourful stickers of the word GREASE, designed like the McDonald's logo. The fashion bandits focus on the real-life histories of, say, Marie Carangi, a famous *Vogue* cover girl, who ended up addicted to heroin, suffering from AIDS and dying in a welfare hospital. Another jamming device is 'subvertisements', like the TV spot created for Greenpeace, called Autosaurus, featuring a model dinosaur constructed of old cars. The huge wreck collapses in a heap, while a voice intones: 'It's coming . . . it's coming . . . the end of the automotive age.' This ad was booked to appear on CBC's Saturday afternoon slot, *Driver's Seat*, but was pulled at the last minute. Why is this surprising? Those at the top of the heap are too happy with present realities to foster alternative ones. It's golden goodness for ever, if not the golden goose, and we must never mention the weather in Cairns.

Those who believe that TV has no impact on consciousness should see how a five-year-old reacts to the ad for Sprinkl'ns, a 'flavoured dairy snack'. It depicts kids in space who claim to have 'strained our brains' to invent the stuff. Barely out of her nappy, my cherub ran berserk in K Mart to find a pack to put on the trolley. She tore into it, after her evening gruel of lentils, while Mum read aloud the ingredients: 'Thickeners, vegetable gums, artificial colours, sugar, starch . . .' After three teaspoons of the pink gooey stuff, the cherub said her stomach hurt, and she put it back in the fridge. Now here's where it gets interesting.

No one else is allowed to taste it, nor open the rest of the containers. (It's sold in packs of four.) The cherub loves her Sprinkl'ns even though they make her sick. It stems from a vision she once saw – kids singing in cyberspace – and now Sprinkl'ns are locked in her heart, and in the family fridge, never to be devoured. To love them, and yet to hate them, all at the same time. In the old days, only a poet would reach such an exalted state of consciousness. (*Odi et amo* . . . I love you and I hate you: Catullus.) Or a victim of reefer madness. Now all it takes is a catchy jingle, an alert toddler and the juggernaut of mass marketing.

(*Resurgence*)

Technicians of Ecstasy
24

In the early nineties, when I first saw Mondo 2000, *with its mind-stretching visuals and cranky prose, I dubbed it the successor to* London Oz. *Later, stumbling through cyberspace on a T-model Mac, I found the Zine scene as refreshing as the early days of the underground press. Is this the rebirth of a counter-culture, I wondered, or the eve of marketing bonanza? This was written before the appearance of* Wired.

1993:

The brilliance of the human brain is its capacity to absorb contradictory notions without upsetting the owner. I can prattle about the futility of progress while stacking the dishwasher. Ethereal vegans claim the world is on the brink of an apocalypse, while lashing out on cosmetic dentistry.

I've never found money interesting, despite qualms about facing old age in a Sandy Stone dressing-gown crouched over a one-bar radiator, while the Hell's Angels embezzle my pension cheque. As a teenager, the Beat Generation put me off the whole idea of a retirement plan. Silly, isn't it? Too much Jack Kerouac at an early age. All I ever wanted was a black duffle coat and a bus ticket to Marrakesh. Tragic. Even if I did pull it off for about twenty years.

Then came kids – the cash ran out and world politics turned into a series of lectures on inflation. Clever friends who had never heard of Lawrence Ferlinghetti started getting Seriously Rich. Even the stubbornly hippie-ish decided to upshift. The backpacker who started off publishing maps of the world's best hash dens is now a travel guide king in a Ferrari. Is he happier?

Probably not, according to Ed Deiner from the University of Illinois, who has 'proved that extra income spawns negative effects'. While a pay rise may briefly boost the recipient's level of happiness, 'the glow fades as the goals start to change'. Life gets messy, friendships fade, every shadow seems like a burglar and book-keeping is a Byzantine maze.

As soon as these findings were published, I realized that the Beats – like the Beatles – would be reborn. Not in the smoky jazz cellars of Greenwich Village, but in the electronic underground of cyberspace, 'the net'. Sure enough, casting my modem into stellar orbit, I captured the world of zines – a phalanx of feisty online journals produced for fun and aimed at the overthrow of Western civilization.

According to the manifesto from *HI-REZ*, the electronic journal for Cyber-beats:

'we BURN in sticky floored 2 in the morning all night coffee houses ripe with APOCALYPTIC VISIONS and we rave at dawn in crumbling 1700s farmhouses. we sizzle along the asphalt veins lacing the skin of the nation together in white high-finned cadillacs driven by madmen. We modulate the very aether itself with ecstatic rf emanations from beat loft radio studios. We are the cyber-beatniks . . . the DANGEROUS NEW ARTISTS . . . the

TECHNICIANS

OF ECSTASY

and
    we

             are
       all
             ENMESHED IN THE NET

stuck together

       by

                    the

       sweet and sticky
                    text characters

that form the dimensional glue

       of this here cyberspace . . .

   we do not FIT the stereotypes and posings of pop
subcultures: we are ALONE in our
art theatre magic alchemy yet we are TOGETHER

       here

       the . . . CYBER-BEATS! . . .'

And so on. The rest of the text is rich with poetry, jokes
and rage, as if the ghost of Jack Kerouac was acid-tripping
at a convention of hackers. The list of zines is never-ending
– BLINK, a forum for the intersection of consciousness and
creativity, FUNHOUSE, a cyberzine of degenerate pop culture,
POWER TO THE PEOPLE MOVER concerned with unusual
and noteworthy behaviour observed on mass transit systems,
particularly the bus lines.
   Zines need not be approached with the grown-up solemnity
required for consuming the dreary fare at your local newsagent.

One's irony antennae should be finely tuned, as in the case of the letters to this Zine Agony Uncle:

'Dear Doctor Avalanche – How do I decide which shade of black to wear with which kinds of days? Deep black for rainy days? Shiny black for sunny days when I can't avoid them? Should I mix shades? Help. Afraid of a fashion faux pas.

Dear Afraid – This is a question indeed worthy of merit. There are two distinct ways of solving this problem. 1) Allow chaos to dip her lovely hand into your life by dressing in the dark. If your wardrobe contains the proper elements (i.e. no item of clothing which reflects any wavelength of the visible spectrum) this should result in a delightfully stylish yet utterly uncalculated personal fashion. 2) Alternatively, never go out before sunset. (My own solution.)'

Inevitably, the freshness and wry wit of the zine scene is transmuting into glossy mags with big name ads, of which the most notable is *Mondo 2000*, published in Berkeley California. Its vibrant columnists promote smart drugs, online anarchy and monkey-wrenching the media, at the same time as they are pursued and promoted by the very media they ridicule, including the *New York Times*. It's the wondrous world of self-contradiction. Hating capitalism, until the expression of rage finds a market and makes a rich capitalist.

(ABM)

Town Houses, 25 Robber Barons

To aging alternative types, Byron Bay is a sacred site – the heart of the rainbow region. Now, this eastern-most tip of north coast New South Wales – a former whaling port, surfing mecca and pscillocibyn hot-spot – is fast becoming the St Tropez of the southern hemisphere. Naturally, I'm not amused.

1993:

It's a shock to take a holiday break to a cheerful and exotic place, and yet remain within your own borders. As the world's first baby boomer, I helped pioneer the hedonistic plunge into foreign shores, opening up the beaches of Bali and the girlie bars of Thailand to the horrors of mass tourism. Three decades later, with the jails of Asia packed with Aussie junkies and bar-keepers, I found myself loading the family car and heading north to Byron Bay, jewel of the 'rainbow region', the last redoubt of hippiedom, the current prey of developer barons.

It is a long day's journey through architectural disarray and brand name mantras along the Pacific Highway, past dispirited malls and sad sack cafés, to reach the beach-ringed knob of Byron, the mainland's eastern-most point. Here, cruising the rolling fields, a flood of memories – a first trip on magic mushrooms, a girlfriend lost to an Adonis-surfer, the Aquarius Festival in 1973, which launched this area as the molten core of a counter-culture that never died.

'Hippies always find the best spots,' a developer roars to

his mates at the Byronian Café, and goes on to describe how he once 'cleaned up' in Ibiza. Indeed, the atmosphere of this onetime whaling port and dairy town evokes heyday Ibiza, blended with the sartorial style of backpacker Asia, and upmarket pub culture.

People look happy. Couples canoodle on the main street, children maraud the ice-cream parlours and flamenco guitars echo from the tapas bar. This is a surprise for a visitor from the Blue Mountains, where the mood is set by dole-queue eyes and pensioner flannels.

In the early seventies, when I first chugged into town in a Valiant station-wagon, it was a place of NOT DOING. Like white Aborigines, lured by the spirit of the place, we just wanted to soak it up; to eat the mushrooms and gaze at the sunsets through tea-tree lakes, prolonging our stay till the money ran out.

'Don't bring your city ways here,' I was scolded on my first day, fumbling with a key-ring. 'No one locks their cars in Byron.'

Gold-skinned in our sarongs and thongs, we consumed Van Morrison in the dunes and wore World-block on our minds; the height of hippie hedonism. At a party, with salad and champagne served from wheelbarrows, we watched home movies of the hosts' last trek to the Himalayas. Their children frolicking, sherpas beaming, the blocks of hash stacked into backpacks . . .

The rains came; we drifted back to the city and wondered about those who stayed behind, chain-sawing the cobwebbed walls of farmhouses to turn them into plate-glass pleasure domes.

A silly place, we decided, a folly of youth; but the beacon kept blinking as the years went by, and older versions of ourselves returned to see the yuppiefication of our former dreamland. Town houses, film stars, robber-barons.

But it wasn't all bad. No skyscrapers or car yards, like

the rest of the north coast. And the abattoir, where once I had smuggled in cameras to catch the death-throes of its inmates, was now a tangle of Macs; an electronic link to a global grid of eco-warriors. A stay-behind surfer had turned into a psychedelic glass-blower; a former *Oz* seller from Stoke Newington now ran a happy-go-lucky pizza parlour. There was rainforest architecture, a radical environment centre, ecstasy encounter groups, 'Bliss-shoes' and a school for the children of the mystically enhanced.

The last frontier was coming down; the most deadly of them all – that boundary between making a living . . . and making a life. For all its psycho-babble and the zonked-out shop-fronts of dolphin-rainbow-Tarot, how boring and desecrated the rest of the coast by comparison. How stuck in the rut of a materialist hell.

And here lies the danger. The more distinctive the atmosphere, the more prone to defilement. Byron is the scene of a clash between commerce and consciousness; which can only be reconciled if the former is tamed and the latter is raised.

The town is on the cusp. The traffic is building, the bank queues are lengthening and the estate agents are locked into a vision outmoded: pack 'em in in; kerbing & guttering. Jobs. Progress. The Joy of Concrete. And You Don't Mess with a Recession. The carpetbaggers are pushing to turn Byron into everywhere else, leaving us nowhere else.

If only the Greens could book every councillor/developer into a condo in Majorca, within a whiff of the septic salt spray, the diet of pom pub grub, the rubbish-strewn stucco malls, disco-muzak, yob-throngs, lager loutism and the lack of Spanish soul. Trouble is, they might like it.

The shadow of Club Med hangs over many a brunch. It's down to the courts and a hit list of endangered species. Frog against frog. I wish I could name a far-away village in another country which has become a 'must-see' because of its proximity to a Coppertone-splathered Cinzano-swilling stockade a-jigging to Le Heavy Metal. Some say it's a matter of working-with-'em, they're here anyway ... Let's design self-sustaining solar-powered mud huts with ten recyling bins and side trips to Nimbin, cooking up bush-tucker soufflé with profits rushed to dolphin research and rainforest regeneration, and don't mention Muraroa.

The notion of progress, as measured by economic growth, is recent and arbitrary; a cultural hallucination – the wealth of nations is the health of the bottom line; our self-worth equals our net worth. Who's measuring leisure, laughter, the taste of tomatoes or whether we have to lock our doors at night?

The point is not to live dangerously, so we can produce prize-winning paintings or prose; but to think dangerously, so we can transcend the pitfalls of corporate excesses, and make the world safe for its inhabitants, down to the last gnat. Byron Bay is precious because its unique spirit has attracted a population that knows this already.

(Byron Bay Holiday Guide)

26
Flattened on the Super Highway

. . . even before I left home. Weary of my own fascination with the media, and aware of the billions of hours stolen from everyday life, I stumbled upon a new disease.

1994:

Now that the whole world fits in a satellite dish, hideous new ailments are striking down baby boomers. Media Alzheimer's Disease (MAD) is one of the quirkiest, and scariest, with the potential to slash profits in publishing, TV, cinema and the entertainment industry. It starts small, as in my case, with the breaking of a lifelong habit of reading the morning newspaper. Later, it can progress to a terminal disinclination to see any of the Top Ten movies, *Larry King Live* or *The X-Files*. It's a cruel, embarrassing forgetfulness to consume the media, which targets former fanatics, and is not susceptible to drugs, electro-therapy or counselling.

At first, you tell yourself it doesn't matter, or that it's a temporary aberration. In my case, two factors combined to trigger the onset of MAD. Deadlines put time at a premium, so I started losing my grip on party political nuances in Tasmania, let alone in Uzbeckistan, and felt hazy about the who's who of gangsta rap. Worse was to come. One Thursday, I failed to buy the morning newspaper. Instead of a guilty, rudderless ignorance sapping my spirit, a cheeky flood of euphoria filled up the afternoon; an incredible lightness of being.

A week later it happened again, only this time for two days – the early symptoms of MAD. Somewhere a child had been tortured to death for three weeks by his father, and I was not appraised of the details. A gender studies student was probably suing her mother for forcing a breast into her mouth as a baby, instead of the preferred option, a bottle – or was it the other way round? – and its significance would never be expounded for my benefit.

Eventually, a friend will spot the warning signs of media forgetfulness, and rub the victim's face in it. 'Ho, ho, so you didn't twig to the Stock Market rumble in Tokyo?' Then comes denial, or a feeble excuse: 'Hey, what's the point of all this information, if I can't act on it?' Or a soppy, New Age rejoinder: 'Maybe it's better to play Snakes and Ladders with the kids than plough through the *Modern Review*.' If the ailment was confined to the print scene, the patient could still muddle through. Alas, MAD is multi-media.

One sultry afternoon at the cinema, I finally lost my marbles. For a stint of movie reviewing, to feed the appetite of another medium, I was obliged to see two blockbusters in a day. During the second one came a bolt from the blue: 'What am I doing here?' Sure, I wanted to slaver over a sexpot wrapped around a pole, like everyone else, but at the cost of a whole afternoon, plus parking fee? Instead of unravelling the intricacies of the plot, I worried about the billions of hours that Hollywood has stolen from humanity's everyday life. How we have convinced ourselves of the vital importance of spending decades in dark halls, held sway by the fantasies of strangers. Philosophers from Heraclitus to the Hindus have argued that human existence is a veil of illusion, and the purpose of life is to strip it away. Movies are an illusion within an illusion.

Perhaps it all started with *Battleship Potemkin*. Seeing it for the first time hurled us into the thick of the history. It saved us from reading the books, learning the language or travelling on the Trans-Siberian Express. Ever since, on a subliminal level, millions now imagine that *Batman Three* could be an updated *Potemkin* in disguise.

It takes about forty years to lose heart. In the days before I was afflicted with MAD, and hired the odd tape, I was amazed by the bombardment of trailers – excerpts from sixty-eight features that no one would want to see in a lifetime, not even on fast forward. Where now are these tapes – seething in landfills?

Next stop, cyberspace. Interactive, global, sexually safe. After the intro razzle dazzle of a million minds flashing on the Mac, the mastering of electronic hieroglyphs, the fabulous download of hospital floor plans from Norway, you suddenly wonder why it's 4am and you're still in pyjamas eight days later. Farewell Internet.

I joined MAD anonymous. One woman recounted how she had let the virus into her home, by subscribing to the *New Yorker*. It landed on her doorstep week after week, in a polyurethane sheath. The magazines piled up the stairs and spread into bathroom and bedroom, accusingly, like a bulk order of condoms never enjoyed. She dealt with her guilt by denial – shunning all printed matter, even the blue-chip guides to restaurants in Paris. Is there a cure? Scientists and medical schools are working around the clock, funded by media magnates.

Shielded from celebrity gossip, CNN and the latest opinion polls, sufferers represent a tragic throwback to a bygone era. Every day they can be seen feeding the birds, staring at sunsets, strolling botanical gardens, playing with stray children and reciting Wordsworth in cafés – the new underclass, spawned by media overkill.

(*Resurgence*)

Golden Arches 27 on the Bluegums

To simultaneously feel contradictionary emotions has now become so common that it has a special name – to spasm. Super-malls are a great place to refine this art – recoil at babies in pushchairs clutching jumbles of white plastic and credit-card receipts, or warm to the lame and the elderly congregating in cosy nooks over cappuccinos, outwitting loneliness. The next generation can also cause a spasm or two . . .

1994:

The slogan on the smalltown newspaper sums up the schizo-phrenia of our age: Changing Bermagui – but keeping it the same. This is not intended as irony. Perhaps the publishers even believe it is possible, as though they have mastered the paradox of how to keep moving while remaining motionless. Why not? With 150 channels in our living-room, it is natural to want the world. My four-year-old, eager to eat ice cream and a sausage simultaneously, was furious to find she had only one mouth.

The biggest shopping centre in the southern hemisphere is up the road from my mother-in-law's. Its slogan rivals that of the *Bermagui Banner* – 'Imagine Everything You Want'. Really?

On the Easter weekend I drove to its car-park. As I inched the Holden skywards, floor after floor, each one of them full, I marvelled at the attendance records. On this holy weekend during my boarding-school youth, we were herded off to the church. I rode down the escalator from the car-park penthouse in search of medication for asthma, the latest craze among toddlers. Surveying a vista of families weighed down with shopping bags, I realized this was the church – our millennial Dreamtime.

Even the babes in perambulators were clutching at jumbles of plastic bags. The laps of the elderly in wheelchairs were stacked with mighty cartons of dinnerware, cosmetics and fluffy animals. If this is a recession, developers better add another twenty floors before boomtime.

The architecture is cunning. A sea of shops in every direction, including up and down. Tackling other floors involves a two-kilometre hike to find an escalator, by which time you've registered a pulsating array of new products vital to your family's survival. If that's the right word. The pediatrician had given me a list of food additives to avoid – 'asthma triggers' – a sheet of calculus to be decoded in the supermarket. Stocking up for the Easter camping trip, it was almost impossible to find items free of contaminants. Perhaps the asthmatics of today function like canaries in coalmines.

Having got the Ventolin, we headed south to celebrate the Resurrection by the sea. Accompanying us was a teenage relative from Britain, Caspar, a product of Westminster School (old boys: Dryden, Kim Philby, Andrew Lloyd Webber), filling in his 'gap year' before polishing off his education. Several of Caspar's schoolmates are also spending Gap on our shores. For these future rulers of Britain, Oz hits the spot with its 'third world ambience and first world facilities'.

He slept all the way down the coast, having been to an all-night rave party in a Parramatta car-park. As our laden station-wagon wheezed into the fishing port, he stirred. The children's tape, *Home Among the Gum Trees*, was too gruelling for his enhanced sensibilities, so we submitted to one of his own – a black French gangsta-rapper with a long angry spiel about the terrors of trying to be chic.

In Bermagui, a ten-foot marlin is craned up to the dock to be weighed – before being tossed into the town dump. My ten-year-old bursts into tears when I fail to explain the joys of Big Game fish liquidation. The local business campaign to erect a Tourist Attraction has gathered momentum – the world's biggest sundial, built of steel, to be plonked on the headland. As our Holden rolls south towards forest-enclosed beaches, there are new subdivisions and serious road works. Grid-locks of heavy machinery, smouldering tree pyres.

Caspar and I lie on a deserted beach, the kids sorting shells. Amazed at the expanse of untrammelled wilderness, he remarks airily: 'I suppose there'll be Golden Arches here when I come back.'

'How come you and your friends are so fatalistic?'

'There's nothing we can do.' Caspar belongs to the group destined to acquire a huge disposable income, the most targeted segment of society. 'Our likes and interests are created in boardrooms months before we know about them.' In the face of such media pressure, true individuality was impossible and rebellion futile. 'What can we protest against?' Vietnam was the last of its kind – now wars are sanitized and processed by CNN to slot between ads. 'No single factor unites us in dissent,' he sighs, 'there are just little rivulets of temporary style.'

'Come off it Caspar – there's a whole planet to save . . .'

'Sure – we tried to stop them building motorways through the ancient forests in England, but thousands of cops turned up with riot shields.' Their demos against racism were blitzed by tear gas. 'Cops have really got it together these days; they're not blundering around the way they did at your love-ins . . .'

Meanwhile, there are rave parties. Caspar rushed off to the sea with a boogey board, determined to catch the last wave. Perhaps his cold-hearted realism will serve the future better than my sentimentality did in the past.

                                                              (ABM)

28
All the World in a Blender

A die-hard pot-trailer who wants the Third World to stay locked in a faded cliché of inscrutability, chaos and surprise? Maybe.

1994:

Nature is wild and vast in the mountains where I live, but shopping has always been a drudge . . . until the Todarello family arrived. The site for their warehouse was inauspicious – a bleak, windswept car-yard next to a nursing home and a funeral parlour. And there is nothing faddish or romantic about their stock – fruit and veggies – though the range is vast, fresh and inexpensive. The Todarellos conquered the bleak town in the Blue Mountains, west of Sydney, and they did it by putting something special back into retailing.

A crying kid is handed a slice of watermelon, a harassed father of eight is presented with a crate of mangoes. Plump, jovial Mr Todarello bathes each customer in a welcoming smile. No matter that he's driven a few hundred kilometres at 3am that morning to the city markets, packing the trucks himself – he's so happy to see you, that you're alive, that he's alive, that the world still spins around the sun, that you've found time to visit his barn, and that you may do him the honour of sampling, for free, a new batch of dates from Morocco . . . On the anniversary of opening day, the family set up Primus stoves in the aisles to cook batches of pasta for their surprised customers.

Their success is triumphant and well-deserved. It is not concocted at business school or at a brand-name university of Fruitology marketing. It stems from the personality of the family – their instinctive concern for the people who walk through the door. For MBAs, the next logical step is to franchise Mr Todarello. Design a logo, put his beaming dial on to a thousand banana arches, proclaim 'pasta give-aways' and cut a swathe through mall-world. It might even work, as a marketing exercise, but the experience would be fake.

'Oh, that doesn't matter,' says a voice, 'it's the way of the future.'

When Howard Johnson started his US chain of diners back in the Middle Ages, he offered a unique sense of security to the nervous family on the road. Predictability and familiarity. Waitresses in gingham, eggs always scrambled the same way. While this is opposite to my own desires in exotic terrain, I can appreciate its appeal.

These days, we have thousands of mighty brand names and food franchises marching across the globe. It has dawned on McDonalds that India has a peckish middle class of 250 million, which grows each year by more than the entire population of Australia. The Golden Arches are glittering above the minarets. Pizza Hut and Kentucky Fried Chicken are licking their lips and shopping for sites. Why does this make my heart sink? Am I a snob? A nostalgia queen? A diehard hippie who wants the Third World to stay locked in a faded cliché of inscrutability, chaos and surprise? Maybe.

In your mind's eye, create a blender as big as the universe. Pop in the planet Earth and press 'purée'. Yum yum, sure, but it's homogenous pap. The world of the future. One of the cutting blades of this blender is Rupert Murdoch, whose video satellite, Star TV, beams *Santa Barbara*, *The Young Doctors* and MTV into the bazaars of Bombay and the banks of the Ganges. At a recent satellite TV conference in Hong Kong, a programme supplier from the US network NBC 'joked' to the audience: 'We're going to ruin your culture, just like we ruined our own.'

Brand fetish fashion czar Pierre Cardin plans to open fifty

outlets in India by next year. Plastering hoardings with jingoist come-ons – 'Join the Cardin Empire' – he dreams of replacing the ancient sari with shoulder-padded tat and gold-plated dangles. Other brands jostling for middle-class rupees include Kelloggs, PepsiCo, Coca-Cola, Wrigleys, Lacoste, Benetton . . . 'About time,' says a voice. Why should the Indians be denied the Cardin keychain to yuppiedom? If That's What They Want.

Democracy turns out to be a two-edged sword. Great at foiling tyrants, but even better at promoting the tyranny of brand names. While I'm not averse to barking at a drive-in pillar for a pack of Chicken McNuggets, and believe the same rights of convenience should apply to the horse-persons of Mongolia, it somehow shrinks the soul of the world, this ever-advancing stodge. Pepsi, Prozac, MTV . . . Until recently, I believed I was the only member of the human race who felt this way. Then I heard what Dennis Potter, the writer, had called the cancer despoiling his pancreas: Rupert Murdoch.

You'll notice he didn't call it Genghis Khan. This brings me to a concluding anecdote, which may save the world. When Genghis was poised for another bloodthirsty sweep into China, he sent for a sage, who, though elderly, travelled 200 miles on a palanquin to meet the tyrant. The sage taught Genghis to meditate. The ambitions of the tyrant melted away and he withdrew his ravenous hordes.

Gurus are a dime a dozen in India, but super sages are hard to find. Unless they want *Santa Barbara* to replace the *Bhagavadgita*, a holiest of holy better hop on a jet to Hollywood and cool out the global tycoon. As for Mr Todarello, beaming through the stack of pineapples, I hope he doesn't come across this column and get a big head . . . and a logo.

(Resurgence)

Postscript

By 1996, the American TV show *Baywatch* was being shown
in 142 countries, including Iran, Lebanon and Mongolia;
broadcast in fifteen languages to a billion viewers world wide.
Baywatch restaurants are next.

29
To Hell and Back

*Some people enjoy pain, and are thrilled by images
of violence – okay, let's deal with that. Is it the
private turn-on of the director or critic? Or is the
creator making new and illuminating connections?
Subversion alone should be no guarantee of critical
glory. Please discuss.*

1993:

Psychic disarray surfaces in bizarre and frightening ways. Can
the arts depict this trend, without being overwhelmed by it?
It's time to ask new questions; ones which transcend the dreary
debate between censorship and the right to show split pink. Is
the glamorization of sadism linked to anti-social behaviour?
Can consumers and critics, in the light of ecological chaos,
heighten their sense of discernment and make new kinds of
judgements, without galvanizing the ghost of Stalin?

Sado-sexual violence is on the ascendancy in the arts, as in
life; groovy, gothic and fun. It's the imagery of our time.

When Gianni Versace's whip-ladies boogied down the cat-
walk, he was later to crow to the *New York Times*: 'At my
launch there were 200 socialites in bondage.' A Hollywood
producer says he's heard so many proposals for movies on serial
killers that he's 'beginning to feel like a victim'. The juiciest jeans
promotion is a forty-eight-page photo saga of group bondage,
jewel theft and spread-eagled sadism. Proclaims the president of
Request Jeans: 'You don't get anywhere playing it safe.' That's
true, but where in the end do you get to?

We've always had horrors and the deep and majestic

depictions of horrors, like Goya's war etchings; but rarely
consumed as a craze. Yesterday, hula-hoops; today, handcuffs.
What's tomorrow? Cannibalism at the crèche, splatterpunk on
Sesame Street . . .?

Images of graphic violence are so pervasive that they're part
of the scenery. Dropping into the video store with a chirpy
three-year-old in my arms, I was distracted by the corner
monitor: a couple in a car having a clipped conversation with
a garage attendant. Suddenly a shotgun appeared, wham bam,
and the victim's face was squashed tomato. Sadder than the
screen image was the look on the face of the child, one of
dumbstruck horror. I felt like an accomplice. The counter-girl
blushed: 'I'm sorry, most of the new releases are like this.'

Life is violent and repression is odious. It is difficult for an
artist to deal with the real world without acknowledging its
carnage. The response can be authentic and powerful, as in Clint
Eastwood's *Unforgiven*; or it can be grotesque and sensational,
like the remake of *Cape Fear*. There is no absolute. Some readers
would reverse my choice. When customs officers raided twenty
Sydney music stores and seized the boxes of 'death metal', I
didn't feel like quoting Voltaire and hounding the censors.
The music delves into cruelty, self-mutilation and necrophilia
– 'slowly slicing your body/wondering what's inside' – but its
fans swear it has power, soul and therapeutic tendencies. It's
all a matter of irony.

Does fascination with violence and cruelty stem from the
blending of pleasure and pain?

The enslavement of O, in *The Story of O*, was a turn-on
for many free spirits. From the châteaux of literary erotica,
Madonna stormed into the Top 40, the world's first feminist
superstar to laud the joys of being spanked. Pain, exquisitely
inflicted, has a long history in the lover's armoury, but when
it ceases to be consensual, the logical outcome is murder. The
intro images in Madonna's best selling book, *Sex*, are leathery
simulations of S & M, replete with whips, chains, ropes, masks,

collars, urinals and lip-rings. In the end, how consensual is a flick-knife held to the throat . . .?

In exposing her private self to public scrutiny, Madonna's courage is undeniable, and perhaps she forces us to confront our own murky depths. Ironically, this book should please the prudes. A virgin who stumbles across it for the first time is likely to join a nunnery. Perhaps that's Madonna's final goal – the de-eroticization of sex.

A book or a movie which celebrates fascism or racism will rarely be hailed as a work of art. Often so hailed is a work which portrays acts of unspeakable violence and torture with luminous intensity over long duration.

On the release of the mass market paperback, *American Psycho*, I was asked to read it, blabbermouth that I am, and give a quickie opinion. I found the book unfinishable, due to the pounding conjunction of copulation and killing, without merit, wit or integrity. Admittedly, in the hands of Bret Easton Ellis, the sex scenes are steamy and enticing . . . at first. But when the writhing females are scoured and diced with industrial hardware, what is the reader to do? Cut the libido and call for the vomit bag . . . yet valiantly plough on, as urged by our littérateurs? Am I sick? Can't I trust myself? But if you've already got an erection during a sex romp, then might it be dangerous to embroil this arousal with the slash and slurp of a chainsaw meeting flesh? Could the connection be catching? If not in the first scene, then maybe the twentieth. It's surely the way they train torturers.

On a Saturday afternoon in August 1991, a cab driver, Wade Frankum, sat in the Coffee Pot Lounge at a suburban Sydney plaza. After an hour, he stood up, rested a knee on his seat and turned to face two teenage girls in the adjacent booth. Frankum stabbed the nearest girl several times in the back, leaving the knife embedded. From his bag, he extracted an automatic rifle and, at zero range, shot five people dead. Running through the plaza, firing at the ceiling, Frankum claimed another victim at the foot of the ramp. After more shooting, he abducted a woman in a car and then, at the sound of police sirens, ordered her to stop, apologized, alighted and killed himself.

Why did he do it? A Sydney psychiatrist, Rod Milton, was assigned by the coroner to tackle this question. In addition to a string of academic credentials, Milton has toiled for years at the coalface of crime, appearing for the defence and prosecution in various murder trials, as well as writing the personality profiles of arsonists, rapists and serial killers. This by no means renders him infallible, but earns him the right to be heard.

Milton believes that regular exposure to the sight of violence on TV and video (where authority figures 'legitimize its use') may have an adverse effect on vulnerable personalities. Along with the wank mags and the porno video catalogues, which we've come to associate with serial killers, Frankum's flat contained a 'well-thumbed' copy of *American Psycho*, released three months before the massacre. Milton claims this book 'probably had a special appeal for Frankum'. The hero is rich, fit and successful, unlike Frankum, and able to indulge in diverse, costly and disgusting sexual hi-jinks. 'It is easy to imagine Frankum admiring this character and being affected by the book.'

Such a conclusion is not easy to accept by the pop intelligentsia, myself included. Meekly raised at a forum on censorship, it was dismissed out of hand, with the cause of the crime comfortably assumed to rest in the swamp of Frankum's formative years.

In his ninety-page report, Dr Milton rejects this view. Despite his quirks and deficiencies, the profile emphasizes Frankum's 'essential normality'. With mass murder unknown in Australia until recently, Milton is led to an unpalatable conclusion: 'I believe societal factors promoting violence exist now which did not exist previously, and it was these which tipped the balance for Wade Frankum.'

We will never truly know whether *American Psycho* had the

slightest impact on Frankum's decision to slay seven strangers. Marijuana use, fits of depression and neighbourhood squabbles are all a part of the stew. But no matter how committed we are to the circulation of wild and dangerous ideas, or to the latest American fiction, there comes a time to pause in our zest for their promotion. (In the most libertarian families, when the thirteen-year-old daughter walks into the room, the Madonna book is slipped on top of the wardrobe.)

Shortly after the release of Dr Milton's profile on Frankum and the headlines citing his worries over the impact of *American Psycho*, the *Sydney Morning Herald* published a guide to Christmas giving. In its Good Living section, 'A Gift with Words', the critics listed their choice of appropriate books for the season of peace on earth. A local literary beacon recommended that stockings be topped up with *American Psycho*.

An asset valued by many of us is our house, a testament to a lifetime of toil. In the event of a catastrophe, a flood or a fire, the loss can be lessened by insurance. But there is another asset, less tangible, which shelters our doubts from the storm of dissent and warms our predilections in the glow of its hearth – our belief system. While this can't be renovated and updated to keep abreast of the fashions, it can also be threatened by alien forces, be they prehistoric, post-modern or apocalyptic. After a lifetime's investment, we can't afford to see our belief systems swept away, which is what makes us as mad as hell when we're cornered. Those whose views were crystallized in the censorship wars of the sixties decry the possibility that the prolonged and excessive depiction of hideous events in the media could have a detrimental social effect. Nor do they connect this cultural pathology with our ailing environment.

Perhaps the repetition of horror-gore doesn't matter a damn. Fine – each to their own – but isn't it better to weigh up the evidence? Or if the evidence is inconclusive, to examine the pattern of our own responses, to check the artefacts more closely and to cease confusing the repugnance, caution or nausea felt by an increasing number with the jack-booted evils of censorship. Maybe we're engaged in an act of cultural therapy. Sharpening our critical concerns, beyond textual grooviness or special effects, might spotlight the feedback between human behaviour and popular culture; between who we are and what we consume.

I don't believe the media should be restrained because of a few vulnerable sad sacks. My fear is this – that we may all be more vulnerable than we think.

Take the case of TV. It either has no effect or some effect. If it has none, then the ad industry is a hoax. If it has some, then it can either be beneficial, like inspiring viewers to contribute to famine relief, scratching their heads over Wittgenstein, or growing veggies in the back-yard; or it can be bad, like glamorizing violence, promoting racism or implying that women yearn to be raped.

In a study spanning thirty-two years, Leonard Eron from the University of Chicago looked at the impact of television on the behaviour of children. In 1960, Eron tested nearly nine hundred boys and girls from a rural New York State grammar school and found a connection between the violence of TV programmes they selected and their roughness in the playground. Ten years later, the link was stronger. The gentler souls of the original study, who had since watched a lot of violent TV, were now rougher and tougher – even more so than the ones who were originally 'highly aggressive' but had not been so exposed. Later still, when the original subjects were thirty years old, Eron found that those who had more frequently viewed violence as boys had gone on to be convicted of more serious crimes ... plus, they tended to beat their own kids, who, in turn, chose violent programs ...

There is no merit in denying our darker side, as it's bound to burst out in other ways. But there's danger too, in putting it on a pedestal and hiring a publicist.

Cruelty is an aphrodisiac. Some men are so hooked that sex is only plausible if accompanied by rape. Are some so repressed or inept that their libido builds up until the banks burst and an innocent is crushed? That's what we used to think. It was a righteous argument in the fight to free up the means of communication. Let it all hang out. But sexual violence did not disappear with the vestiges of censorship.

Video-porn can incite lust to an astonishing degree. Deep in their hearts, many men admit to reaching a point, with continued viewing, of prurient obsession, from which they pull back in shock and self-disgust. But it's what happens when we don't pull back that worries me.

Since 1985, in the US, reports of child abuse and neglect have increased by 40 per cent. What's going on in the heads of the perpetrators? How have such desires been shaped? Do these atrocities signal an abyss to which we are all capable of succumbing?

In the book *Apocalypse Culture* (Amok Press), the editor argues that the 'aesthetic terrorist' is the last bastion of purity, providing 'an effective counter terror against the insidious mantras of consumerist brainwash'. He cites a magazine from Chicago, *Pure*, a xeroxed zine which extols child torture, murder and extreme misogyny; one which has 'tweaked too many civic minded noses, and its editor, Peter Sotos, was tailed for nine months . . .' Poor diddums. In an interview, Sotos declared: 'I'm a great fan of sexual violence and sadism . . . My tastes run very similar to Ian Brady and I enjoy his work because it is 100% honest and self-concerned. He fucked and tortured little Lesley Downey every way imaginable before smashing her tiny skull . . .' A page reproduced from *Pure* shows headshots of abducted children juxtaposed with ejaculating penises. According to Sotos, his magazine has found its largest readership among those 'involved with or interested in violent electronic music'. In other words, as pop culture catches up, there is an avant-garde pushing further and further into the hellhole.

This is not a debate about free speech and censorship. It is about trying to develop a way to react to our culture which takes into account the health of the culture – an effort to invent holistic criticism. By which I don't mean a chunk of social realism adrift on a sea of environmental platitudes; like a statue of Lenin in a Greenpeace dinghy.

'At the time you're being an artist,' said David Cronenberg, echoing the familiar bravado of the avant-garde, 'you're not a citizen. You have, in fact, no social responsibility whatsoever.' This sounds fine coming from an Oscar 'All art is quite useless' Wilde, actually a moralist, but rings false in the mouths of today's new narcissists.

'What was once a liberating notion,' writes Suzi Gablick, of the art for art's sake credo, 'has become a self-defeating limitation in the new urgencies before us; as a guiding myth, it cannot suggest terms for an alternative, and possibly transformative, practice.' To keep harping on the conflict between the individual and society is no longer relevant, when both are falling apart.

Our boring tenured radicals think they're still at the cultural barricades; defending the bellicose egos of tortured superstars, while they snipe away at 'conservative' pleas for parental stability, social responsibility and the re-enchantment of the arts. But their holy cow of subversion is the Trojan horse of calamity.

When we first saw the world 'as a whole' and realized it was ailing, then the way we viewed our own behaviour altered for ever. Things we had taken for granted were put into question. All kinds of activities, like chucking away a Mars Bar wrapper, sunbathing, flicking on the air-conditioning, felling a tree, fertilizing a field, choosing detergent . . .

Normal, sensible, everyday people stopped buying bigger and better stereos and pitted their energies into Earth repair; from sorting garbage to harvesting the sun. With this shift of perspective came a sensitivity to psychological processes, ones which look at wellbeing, as opposed to dwelling on neuroses. The fruits of this revolution, an emphasis on psychic restoration, are abundantly clear to the attuned observer; seeping into business, medicine, politics, education, diet, recreation, travel and, yes, popular culture. It is a heartening counterpoint to the position of pop nihilism.

But it is up to us, the audience, to discern the difference. Our academics are lost in a spiral of self-referencing technical obscurity, oblivious to the nuances of deep ecology, terrified of breaking rank and hoodwinked by Franco-babble. 'Adopt the perspective further still and accept, for instance, to destroy the belief in truth under all its forms.' Talk about flogging a dead horse. This is not a time for degeneracy, but for regeneration, a time to reconstruct, not deconstruct.

For the most part, the professional critics are in the hands of the industry, seeing themselves as keyboard rebels, but in reality agents of orthodoxy, who rarely say boo to a publicist or repudiate exploitation, egomania or excess. And too modish to admit shock or mystification. Shock can be therapeutic, of course, as with Dickens, Solzhenitsyn or *Apocalypse Now*, if grounded in compassion and reaching for a vision of connectedness with ourselves and the rest of the world.

Lovelock's Gaia hypothesis maintains that it is the activities of humans which have put the world out of kilter, and that it may choose to rescue itself by eradicating us. The Neville hypothesis maintains that popular culture is out of kilter, and that unless we take a stand, looking beyond the whizz-bang-zap-zap, into deeper questions of intention, impact and interconnectedness, we'll sink into a collective slough of narcissism, despair and bloodshed.

If shoppers are capable of rejecting a brand of tuna because of its links with dolphin slaughter, then surely the public is capable of rejecting base-level splatterpunk, if it slaughters our self-respect, promotes aggression or demeans the human condition. I'm not attacking surrealists sweating in garrets, but global empires who cynically pander to easy profits, cheap sensations and reversed priorities.

Feminism thrives on the justice of its case, as did the move to abolish slavery. After years of agitation and argument, we have finally reached a point where corporations can be shamed from fouling a river. It's time to tackle a system which fouls another resource – the river of our dreams, our desires and our collective destiny.

(*The Independent* (Australia))

30
High with a Little Help from My Thongs

Creating bread and curd out of thin air, and poetry out of the mouths of rats.

1994:

A woman who had lost her fortune in the recession and was miserable and angry about it recently took a cheap passage to India. We dreaded her return.

She would gush about the impossible heights of luxury scaled for a pittance in palace hotels, the gorgeous clothes, the fawning, liveried servants, the incredible bargains – all of which would be recycled, remarketed and caricatured with her own logo. Suzette is a nightwear designer. Her latest range of bathrobes would be made from gold embossed saris and shipped to the malls. Showercaps would be designed like turbans. She would lecture *Vogue* readers on simplicity and how bright pink is the navy blue of India. She would sashay through talk shows in jodhpurs from Jodhpur, while *bons mots* in Sanskrit dripped from her lips, glazed with 'Rajasthan Sunset'. Her accountant would be replaced by a guru with an abacus, and her clients would be advised to swap their Laura Ashley sofas for a custom-designed bed of nails.

Maybe the monsoon would close all the ports, we dreamed, and Suzette would be trapped in Calcutta.

But no – she reappeared on schedule. And yes – she had been transformed. Back to her old sweet self again, the one we knew before the eighties came and crushed her smile. It wasn't a new religion, or an ancient breathing technique which did the trick, but the experience of dealing with the daily hassles of India, and seeing how the locals coped. Laughter, fatalism, a crazy joy – the armour of misfortune, as opposed to the hard-hearted bitterness adopted by our own disheartened yuppies. I suddenly missed the sickly labyrinths of Chadni Chowk, the hash milkshakes at midnight, the chit-chat in the gutters with sadhus posing as shoeshine wallahs.

'Don't meditate on pavements while wearing thongs,' I was told on the eve of my last trip, too long ago, 'rubber fumes make you dizzy.' In desert outposts, this is a desirable state, so I packed two pairs. In the Maharaja's palaces, now converted to hotels, I checked the dusty visitors' books. Under 'reasons for coming', the British officers of the Raj had written: 'for the pig-sticking and opium'. This made me feel virtuous, as I had come to Bikaner to visit the shrine of a saint, Karani Matar, who was credited with many miracles, including healing the blind and creating bread and curd out of air.

Although she had died in 1538, Karani was still widely revered, mainly by a tribe of professional poets. On her deathbed (aged 160, reputedly), Karani had told her thousands of followers that they would remain with her at the temple in all their ensuing reincarnations ... as rats. Perhaps she wasn't mad about their poetry. On the other hand, every rat which dies within the precincts of her temple is reincarnated as a Charan poet, giving them a chance to brush up their verse.

The marble temple is like a miniature Moghul palace, with a series of tessellated balconies and courtyards. The saint told the Charan that as rats, they would be worshipped by the people, and she didn't sell them short. On the day of my visit, scores of believers prostrated themselves – groups of oblivious children, mothers cradling babies, a bridal party – while the rats darted across their bodies.

Our guide assured us that no disease had ever emanated from the temple, 'not even during the great plague', and, to be fair, in Hindu mythology the rat is not seen as its real self, but as an abode of Godliness.

A solemn circle of men in black sunglasses sat on the floor fingering beads and hypnotically chanting. These were the Charan poets – still devoted to the saint after all these centuries. It was touching. In Australia, the only thing worshipped by poets is government funding. 'What was your previous incarnation?' I asked a Charan. 'Oh, many, many times a rat,' he replied, and I believed him. His nostrils twitched, his body jerked, his features were distinctly rodentesque. 'So which is better – being a rat or a poet?' Without hesitation, he replied, 'To be born again in this compound as a rat, close to my sacred mother, is my greatest joy.' It was understandable – there are no marble temples for poets.

When I shared this memory with Suzette, she turned it into a line of slippers – whiskers on the toes, a tail stuck to the heel and an Urdu sonnet on the inner sole.

(*Asian Business Review*)

31
Its Legs Still Jerking

The surest way to become the culture czar of a nation, these days, is to start out as a restaurant reviewer. The foodies fly high. Heck, I pine for the time when guys ate anything you put in front of them. Now, the top chefs pay lyrical tributes to offal sausages in the glossies, and dream of seasoning the bangers with their own blood. True. I say . . . a pox on all food snobs.

1994:

Many of my friends from student days have become unspeakably rich. Sometimes they entice me to their favourite eateries, an occasion that fills me with dread. Not because wealth fosters cynicism, a fate some avoid, but because super-expensive restaurants give me the heebie-jeebies. The more upmarket the ambitions of the chef, the more uptight is the mood at the table.

Maybe millionaires have fun in bed, or in speedboats, but in a restaurant they seem to want servility, pretension and exaggerated formality. The other night I was dragged off to the Haughty Cavalier, allegedly the classiest joint in the southern hemisphere, where I was reduced to the brink of suicide. The heavy-metal décor was stunningly hostile, the waiters were stunning. Three sultry beefcakes with flash haircuts, rings in their noses, short jackets and peek-a-bulge pants guided our party to a gloomy alcove suspended near the Harbour Bridge. Strains of Liszt conjured up portraits by Edvard Munch, which the other diners resembled.

The chef, we were firmly informed, was 'in the mood to cook fish tonight'. Yeah – thanks – but suddenly I was in the mood to eat lentils. The breathless prose of the menu would churn anyone's stomach: steamed quail in cauliflower-stuffed nan, wrapped in sun-dried cabbage leaves, dusted with caviar and left to float down the Ganges until it reached Sydney, where it was garnished with Lake Wapengo oysters and served on a bed of organic couscous and braised duck's wings. That was a starter. It cost the same as a round-the-world air-ticket, but no one blinked. Exorbitance is part of the flavour. Patrons are amused by the knowledge that their excreta, ounce for ounce, is worth more than gold.

An element of cruelty is important. The last time I was lured to a high-class clip-joint – the town's finest Japanese – I was compelled to watch my host grind a fork into the belly of a blanched lobster, its legs still jerking. The atmosphere at the Haughty Cavalier and its equivalents is like midnight at the casualty ward. Some couples sit silent, staring into each other's misty champagne. Other tables resound to the false guffaws of Senior Management trying to carouse. In our darkened nook, the women wept openly as they discussed the inroads of Time on their facelifts. The men sent their compliments to the chef, but failed to clean their plates.

Dessert rallied morale. Brows twisted like presidents discussing the disposal of nuclear waste, my companions weighed up the joys of a pickled walnut zabaglione of virgin hen's eggs on a base of spun Tasmanian sugar, versus flambé of mango slices in green ginger pine-nuts served over red Stilton with a privet garnish.

Eating out wasn't always this depressing. Maybe the food snobs have blinded the élite to a sense of fun and adventure. The secret of a great restaurant is not only the food, but the ambience, derived from an uneven mix of clientele. The sneering, dinner-suit-clad waiters of La Coupole in the seventies darted among locals, tourists, celebrities, sex revolutionaries and the downwardly mobile, all barking at each other at once, behaving as though this was the last night out of their lives. Occasionally, it was.

A meal at the Mohti Mahal in Delhi once cost less than the tip for a burger in the West End, but all human life was there, from the beggars at the door to the raga-playing sadhus in the corner, plus leering diplomats, disdainful travel writers, ashram-bound backpackers, jugglers and snake-charmers. It was never the chef who showed off, but the diners.

You think me naïve? Perhaps the whole point of being rich is to insulate yourself from the hoi polloi. It's death by a thousand yawns at the Haughty Cavalier, wondering where the waiters go for a snack, and passing around boxes of Kleenex. That's why the after-dinner mints are supplemented with anti-depressants.

At heart I'm a slummer, preferring the low life to no life. Whether it's the roller-skating waiters in Bangkok, or a seedy jazz café in Marmaris, the ambience is the magic that makes it tick – a feeling that God's in his heaven and the chef has no pretensions to dislodge him. And that the seared pheasant's innards stuffed with sun-dried sheep's eyes are being served at the joint down the road.

(*Resurgence*)

Golden Journey 32 to Samarkand

It took me two years to write my last book,
Hippie Hippie Shake, *not to mention the lifetime*
to live it. The publisher's advance barely covered
the first chapter, and I was too disorganized to
apply for a grant. Still, there's always journalism.
The challenge of accepting an assignment from a
tourist mag is to write between the lines.

1993:

A trek is a trip involving hardship and difficulty, according to the dictionary, so I was wary of taking a nine-year-old. What the hell – my daughter is camel-crazy, thanks to a sumptuous recycling of *Tracks*, the account by Robin Davidson of her epic journey into the interior, and the pamphlet was reassuring – 'Anyone can ride camels on a string.' But where was Kangaroo Island? No one I knew had a clue.

It turns out to be a thumbnail smudge off the South Australian coast, a half hour's flight from Adelaide in a Tiger Moth. From the air, it looks flat and featureless. The dwellings are few, sheep plentiful and trees scarce. On arrival at Kingscote, we were driven to a resort at American River, found in 1895 and handed down through generations, each one adding its own architectural flourish. Styles vary from bush-rock shanty to fifties motel, from pueblo to galvo to fibro, from treated timbers to suburban brick. The resort encloses a salt-water pool, which is huge and inviting, but our timing was off.

'In the opinion of management, the pool is hygienic,' proclaimed the notice. 'However, owing to new health department regulations and a shortage of automatic equipment, the pool is closed.' An afterthought was added in chalk: 'You are welcome to use it at your own risk.' Meanwhile, the jacuzzi beckoned. But on the edge of this turbulent tub, the health department had put its own notice, spelling out its graphic bylaws: No person shall spit, spout water, frolick, permit an animal to enter, blow his nose or urinate . . .

An afternoon stroll seemed the best option.

At 9.30am the next morning, as arranged, I assembled on the track outside the resort with my daughter, Lucy, and Liz, the photographer. Another couple hung about with their bags and a video camera, Horst and Erica, who said they had been given the trek for Christmas. An hour later came this spellbinding sight. Two young bushies leading a string of seven camels towards us, ancient, stately and majestic. 'Udu . . . udu,' they cried, tugging at dusty ropes. Each beast was caparisoned in the traditional manner, evoking the Arabian Nights, and slung with a Waltzing Matilda swag. 'Hooshta . . . hooshta.' The camels stopped and folded to the ground, like oversized deckchairs collapsing in slow motion.

'You'll notice it's all low-tech,' remarked the cameleer, John, as he roped our gear to their sides and indicated the twelfth-century design of the saddles. Apart from an 'ageing delinquent', Cooper, No. 4, we were told that the camels were reasonably friendly, so long as we didn't approach them flapping our hands. Unfortunately, because of the load, not everyone could ride at once. My daughter mounted – 'Ibna . . . ibna . . .' – and shot jerkily into the air, beaming. Patrick, the second cameleer, led the string along the sandy shores of the bay, as tourists aimed their videos, gulls flapped and pelicans hovered.

> Away, for we are ready to a man!
> Our camels sniff the morning and are glad.
> Lead on, O master of the caravan:
> Lead on the Merchant-Princes of Baghdad.

Walking behind, as light as air, I was thrilled to be striking into the heart of this alien island. 'Once inhabited by unknown native people', according to the resort map, 'who became exinct before the white man came'. Extinct? Or did they just move to the mainland? Perhaps this tribe knew something we didn't. Our destination was Anxious Cove.

The track pushed through clumps of scrub, eucalypts, malee and broome bush, which the camels wrenched with their teeth as they passed. And what big teeth they have. Especially Cooper's. I learned that on the previous trek, Cooper had bitten a tourist's knee, 'quite badly', which I presumed was outback jargon for 'never walk again'. Another tourist was knocked to the ground by a branch, although she eventually regained consciousness. No wonder the brochure advised a 'personal accident policy'.

As the scrub thinned, I saw that the ground was littered with bones – bleached thighs, spines, skulls, ribs, even an intact skeleton. Stragglers, perhaps, from previous treks. A goanna scampered behind a clump of blackboys. John said the root of this shrub contained a chemical formerly used in the making of explosives. A veteran of mainland treks, his reverence for camels was boundless: 'If someone attacked them, I'd fly in boots and all.' And sure, Robin Davidson was 'pretty gutsy'. (Her book was a boost for business.) Two more goannas crossed our path, and I watched for peacocks and turkeys, both roaming wild. Just as the caravan was hitting its stride, it was noon – lunchbreak.

The others dismounted and we set about gathering firewood, then changed our minds. It was too windy. The cameleers buttered the bread and laid out the processed meats, while we chopped up Kraft cheese, tomatoes and cucumbers; washed down with lime cordial. Then I was put on the back of Bejah, leader of the string, a 'thorough gent', who was known to be cautious and wise. Like its rider. 'Ibna . . . ibna . . .' In three quick sweeps I was on top of the world, whoosh, then snug in the saddle as though I was born there.

Behind me, Lucy sat on a beast called Bliss, a name appropriate to its rider's mood. Not even the flick of eucalypt twigs in her face, as Bejah's fodder rebounded, deflated her ecstasy. Our string skirted the coast from the top of a hillock, then trod down a steepish, thin, wooded track. Not too far down, though, because Bejah came to a halt. Despite Arabic pleas of encouragement, he still wouldn't budge.

Bits are not used on camels, as their mouths are endlessly munching. Control is exerted by a carved peg placed in a nostril; a look which is bound to sweep the discos. But Bejah, indifferent to tugs on the peg, had transcended the realm of pleasure and pain. 'What now?' asked Patrick, uncharacteristically vocal. The scrubby corridor was too thin for a U-turn, and the camels couldn't walk backwards. Bliss nuzzled my knee, ever more hungrily, so I slipped her an apple. We just sat there.

As perplexed as he was, John was not angry. This sensitive bushie had too much respect for Bejah's experience. The camel was making a decision on behalf of the whole group, he reasoned. The track was unfamiliar. Perhaps Bejah sensed danger. Or perhaps he was too old to make the grade. In any event, we plunged sideways through the scrub, the branches pressing hard against our ankles, and found a way to the shore by another route. 'Udu . . . udu . . .' All too soon, about 3pm, we had reached our campsite, Anxious Cove.

The tide was low, the shore was rocky, the swim was bracing. Summer temperatures on the island are eight degrees cooler than Adelaide. Patrick chucked out a line and Lucy collected thick chunks of cuttlefish, which she carved into profiles of camels. The fire was set in a lonely patch of sand and we circled it with our swags. The cask wine flowed. Cooper was loathed by the other camels, John said, for being such a jerk. In the outback, another camel, Charlotte, had once tried to kill him. It was then that I learned of the lesbian separatists.

Charlotte, who has a huge square hump, is known to mount other females. What's more, she tries to break away from the pack and form her own herd. Charlotte once floored Cooper by biting his ankle. Then she sat on his neck with the full weight of her body, choking him. It's what camels do to humans, when they're cross. John beat off Charlotte with a fence post. Another camel, Delilah, a 'butch dyke' . . . but why go on? This is a family trek. As the sun sank behind the scrub, the full moon rose over Anxious Bay.

The first course was whiting and trevally, thanks to a passing launch, followed by a green salad. Then came slabs of rump the size of doormats and twice as thick. It was tender and juicy, like meat remembered from childhood. Horst and Erica, who had sailed to Australia thirty years ago and found fame as pastry-cooks and chocolate-makers, reckoned it was the steak of the century. A stingray flapped to the rocks to scrounge the scraps.

Leaving the others to carouse, Lucy and I unrolled our swags under the clouds. In the morning, it was yet another feast of traditional protein, bacon and eggs, which left me puzzled as to why none of us ate this way at home. The dolphins frolicked nearby. Lucy found the spiralled egg of a shark. As we lashed our swags to the saddles, I studied the camels more closely. To my horror, Leonora, the talkative one with the lecherous lips, looked a lot like me. I hoped my breath wasn't as foul. 'Ibna . . . ibna . . .'

In next to no time it was lunchtime. Patrick revealed that he often led treks for the weight-watchers, but I didn't believe him. This was a stroll for anorexics in recovery. Back in the saddle of Bejah, I perked up. It is something to do with a rolling vibration under the loins, at a nurturing rhythm, that only men will understand. Flocks of galahs, a baby wallaby. I was just settling in for the afternoon, when the unique façade of the resort heaved into view. Alas, it was not a mirage.

Next trek, give me a year in the Hindu Kush, on short rations.

(Holiday)

33
The Prince of Penturbia

For its first issue, a magazine called Home Office *wanted me to extol the virtues of the cyber frontier. A new arena for fully adult play, for developing creative strategies for the self, for achieving a new kind of becoming? More like a lifetime of pizzas and dirty pyjamas.*

1994:

I've always been an early adopter. A walking target market. Perhaps it comes from being the world's first baby boomer, owing to my father darting home from the war ahead of his regiment, and everyone else's regiment, and my mother being pleased to see him. It's an awesome responsibility, being the First Boomer, as my personal pattern of consumption sets the global trend. The first disposable razor was test-marketed at Santorini, Greece, in December 1975, to take advantage of my presence on the island. Market researchers, pasty in their tourist disguises, lurked in the cobbled square, pens poised. Would Neville buy a Bic? Would he commit a Repeat Purchase? Yes, and yes. The rest is history.

It was the same with Walkmans, Filofaxes, frisbees and solar-powered fan-cooled pith helmets. Quite a responsibility.

As soon as the silicon chip was invented, and a fax machine was available for leasing, I pawned my mother's jewellery and set up the World's First Home Office. This move into rural retreats by urban smarties was briefly called 'penturbia' (pen=5), the fifth wave of migration after settlement, town, city and suburbia: 'twenty acres and a modem'. Instead of harvesting wool or wheat and taking the bales to market, the new settlers would harvest words and ideas and fax them to the brain cells of a grateful metropolis.

But no one had told the high-tech nerds about weather. Our first fax, a NEC console the size of a Jeep, was a lightning attractant. It sucked the bolts out of the sky and sent Death-Row voltage through the Home Office and nearby facilities, such as schools, fire stations and hospitals. A stroke of Japanese genius. Our blender, photo-copier and a fish-tank pump were turned to molten lava. Penturbia is a great place for harvesting ideas, but a nightmare to get anything fixed.

Now we've acquired a costly array of circuit-breakers, surge-busters and insurance policies. At the approach of a cloud, every device is switched off and unplugged, while my wife lights the candles, writes out the day's invoices and prepares a family meal on a Primus. By which time I've completed the disconnections and the threat has passed.

Once you've set up the Home Office, you cannot afford to hire a secretary. Thus, you become the secretary. And the office cleaner. The fun keeps snowballing. No more hearty lunches with mates at the poolside. Now, it's a snack at the desk while you top up the toner. No sick pay, no holiday pay, no overtime, and no free paperclips. The Home Office is the twenty-four-hour office, thanks to international time-zones. The kids are in bed, you've turned off the Xerox. Bip, bip, bip. London calling. It's a fax from the Ideas Market . . .

At first it all feels wonderful, standing at the crossroads of the Global Interface, re-inking the printer ribbon. At dawn you potter about in your dressing-gown, peeling off the faxes while you wait for the kettle to boil. Life in the fast lane. The Prince of Penturbia. King of the silicon chip road. Soon you'll project into hyperspace, and flirt with virtual entities. You'll thrive in a galactic cyberia packed with art and high-tech, credit and information, pop culture and subcultures. Freed from linear time, you will greet the exponential explosion of time with ecstasy, thrilling to new forms of communication, new philosophies, new art, new politics, new realities. Your mindstyle is now – flashing, dense, binary, supersonic, faster than light. Only you haven't managed to leave home. Not for about a year.

With the office next to the bedroom, you don't need to get out of your pyjamas. In cyberspace, there are no dress codes. OK, so you try to maintain standards, and slip on a Dacron tracksuit and Ugh boots, in case the paper supplier drops by. But why tart yourself up? The penturbian's ideas might circle the globe, but his body rarely gets spotted in public. As the years go by, old friends phone to ask how you're enjoying retirement.

I had once dreamed of the integration of work and play, home and family life, as achieved by artisans in the eighteenth century. On Dad's knee, the son of the master carpenter learns how to knock up a wardrobe from the age of five, as the daughters slap varnish on the mahogany, in between milking the cows and studying astronomy. After the jolly evening venison, the family sings rustic songs by the fire, while quaffing a keg of mead. But it's not as easy as it sounds. I'm always at home for my kids all right, as a brooding figure in rags hunched over the keyboard eating yesterday's pizza, and barking at editors.

Then there's the treadmill of the eternal upgrade. However fancy your gadgetry, it will be obsolete by the time of the first lease payment. In the press, a team of salespersons posing as journalists try to make you feel like a blacksmith; unless you upgrade every Monday. The age of computers is capitalism's finest hour. It offers the illusion of freedom at the price of conspicuous consumption.

Missing most from the Home Office is the camaraderie of café or pub that occurs between workplace and kitchen sink. The Third Place. Back in Greece, this was the alcove of the temple, where the old codgers invented philosophy. Or in the cafés of Paris, where they dreamt up ways to make the rest of us feel stupid. It's a good time to buy coffee futures, because in the backwoods of our nation, the blossoming penturbias, cappuccino bars are springing up like er, cappuccino bars; even in the Blue Mountains, where we're still getting to grips with the spelling. The Third Place. A home away from the Home Office.

(Home Office Magazine)

34
Tots, Toothpicks and Tampons

Blackboard Jungle *is tamer than* The Lion King,
Easy Rider *is cuddlier than the school bus. Trapped
in the generation gap at fifty.*

1994:

Renting a video is a way to reclaim the past, as well as keeping
your child amused on a wet weekend. My eleven-year-old
daughter was ready for *West Side Story*, I felt, even though it
was considered gritty and daring in 1961, the time of its release,
and hailed as a 'controversial masterpiece'. *West Side Story* is a
musical set in Manhattan, with racist cops and warring youth
gangs, based on the tragedy of Romeo and Juliet. The Jets, a
gang of blue collar Anglos, is battling to hold its turf from
Puerto Rican invaders, the Sharks. Talk about a fine bunch
of lads – these days, parents would trip over themselves to get
their kids into either of these support groups.

The big bad Jets wear tailored windcheaters and dry-cleaned
chinos. Their hair is short, neat, natural. The Jets are proficient
at basketball and ballet-dancing. Despite growling at ebony-
hued invaders, they do not employ terms of racial abuse. The
Sharks are even more impressive, with shiny suits, slicked-down
hair and stylish pumps. They uphold family values and seek
steady employment. Both gangs confine their courtship to the
opposite sex, eschew tattoos and burst into soppy love songs.
Our small town in the Blue Mountains, west of Sydney, would
be proud to host the Jets and the Sharks for a weekend rumble,
but no one would come.

All the kids are down at the BodyArt franchise getting their nipples pierced. Within ten minutes of *West Side Story*, my daughter was yawning. 'I thought you said this was about street gangs,' she whined, as the leader of the Jets cha-cha'd across a crowded dance floor. Then Natalie Wood had a slanging match about the state of her neckline. She wanted it lowered an inch. Do you hear that, Madonna? One inch! Anyway, she lost the argument and my daughter ejected the tape.

'A policeman rides on the school bus now,' she said.

'That's good, dear. Is he teaching you the road rules?' Puppet shows, a cute jingle – Stop, Look and Listen – I could imagine the scene. She's only in junior school, but you can't start too early.

'Don't be silly, Dad. It's to stop the kids up the back having punch-ups.' Last week, one boy was knocked out. 'Or maybe it's the dope.'

'What's that, dear?'

'Oh, Dad! Where'vya been? Cigarettes made from incense.' The back of the bus, she said, usually smelt like a temple in Bali.

These aggro kids, I should emphasize, are from the Other School. At my daughter's genteel academy, the playground is pacifist. The lessons are touchie-feelie; yoga, tie-dying, star-gazing. Her classmates are called Harmony, Ashtar, and Pleiades. The school motto is 'Go Planet!'. The fifth form band plays Purple Haze and the choir's entire repertoire is drawn from *The Van Morrison Songbook*. There's no school uniform.

That's why the Other Kids are so vile. I mean, if you had to sit in the back of a bus in flannels and a regimental tie, trying to master geometry, while the hippie kids clambered aboard with their mini-skirts and nose-rings, all humming 'The Times They Are A-Chang'n', wouldn't you want to take a big hit of incense? And then take a big hit at the guy dripping with peace signs who was poking fun at your aura?

If you remade *West Side Story* in Australia, it would be the Loggers versus the Forest Ferals. Today's gang warfare has moved out of the cities and into the rainforests. The Loggers fight for their livelihoods, their towns and the rights of Japanese gourmets to pick their teeth with our old-growth eucalypts. The Ferals are nomadic and communal, flitting among the tree ferns in their dreadlocks, living in tepees, bursting into Main Street to demonstrate against roads, tree-felling and Club Med. At one demo in northern NSW, female Ferals marched naked against the hard-hats, ochre-daubed with used tampons dangling as earrings; a comment on consumer waste. (Serious green menstruators now promote sphagnum moss as the solution to feminine hygene.) The dozer drivers didn't know which way to turn. The old-time country coppers did their best, but have all sought transfers to the city.

Anyway, I didn't give up with my daughter, just because the Jets and the Sharks failed to cut the mustard. She wants it tough, huh? Okay, so I hit her with the flick that started it all – riots in the back stalls, a generation in revolt, the Pill, *Sergeant Pepper*, Nixon dragged from the White House . . . 'Fasten your seat belt,' I said, pressing 'play' on *Blackboard Jungle*.

She smirked. 'What's that the teacher's wearing?'

'A sports jacket . . .'

'And that thing he's drawing on?'

'A blackboard . . .' It was useless. The hoods looked quaint. A pair of sneakers doesn't have the same sense of menace any more. 'Okay, you choose,' I said, 'but a classic.' She put on a childhood favourite, *The Cook, The Thief, His Wife and Her Lover*, while I went outside to look at the stars.

(*The Guardian*)

35
Baby You Can Light My Fire

After the devastating bushfires of 1994, which almost destroyed my family's home, I sat down, sleepless and weary, to write the unofficial record. And suddenly the sex-war flared up.

1994:

After twenty-five years of being battered by feminism, the Australian male was a pathetic figure as he lurched into the New Year. Fat and sedentary, he had lost his confidence – in the boudoir, in the office, in the locker-room. (Female reporters won the right to interview jocks in the showers.) Even guys like me were a mess; the ones who could mash carrots, make a stab at finding the G-spot and burst into tears when they couldn't find a parking space.

From the frontlines of social change, women cited statistics to demonstrate their oppression, dumped the kids with 'Dad' and dashed off for urgent consultations with Tibetan lamas and hair colourists. Then the bush fires came.

The Missus got very quiet. We were holidaying by the sea, 400 kilometres south of our home in the Blue Mountains, when the fires hit the headlines. I was mopping the floor, flipping the pancakes and wondering if I should put my hair in rollers, when the call came through from the house-minder. 'Nothing to worry about,' came a tense voice, 'funnels of black smoke on the horizon.' That night, as I polished the bedroom mirrors and ironed the linen, I assured my wife it would take more than a few flames encircling our isolated home for me to abandon the family holiday, rush back and leave her alone with two children, her mother, several house guests and feminist neighbours.

By Saturday morning, the fires had worsened. The house-minder had fled, the road to the Mountains was closed, 'except to residents', and the Little Woman started to worry about her photos, especially the ones of old boyfriends. 'I'll rescue them,' I said jumping into her mother's delightful two-seater runabout, as My Better Half – get this! – packed me a hearty cut lunch and a Thermos of coffee. Six hours later, after inching through police road blocks, I was zooming along the Great Western highway, wondering why all the traffic headed the other way, tugging trailers of furniture. Sirens blared, the sky was pink and ash blotted the windscreen. Maybe the whole State was on fire? On ABC radio – pulse of a nation – the focus was elsewhere. The *Coming Out Show* delved into the latest lesbian-oriented translation of medieval Persian quatrains.

That night I slept alone, circled by a distant ring of burning cliffs. In the morning, my helpmate called from her resort to say that nearly a hundred houses had been lost overnight, and the experts advised home-owners to stay put and fight the inferno, but could I please first evacuate the lounge suite, a wardrobe, the paintings, a few trunks of clothes and the best china? I put on big boots, a hard hat and plastic goggles. By nightfall, the house was fortified and my consort's bric-à-brac was stacked in the runabout. Just as I was about to take a breather, a gang of men in bright yellow overalls burst into the room and asked to borrow the tea-towels. A Mountain men's group? Pointing to a rapidly approaching sheet of flame, they wrapped the towels around their faces – as did I, feeling like a Lone Ranger, though not alone.

From then on, it was the whir of water pumps, the screech of saws, the crackle of singed eucalypts. Soot tarred our flesh, smoke got in our eyes. We spat, we cursed, we lit a few fires of our own – strategic backburns – and we aimed our big long nozzles at the shimmering bush. A cock crowed, hoses spurted, intercoms crackled. Black-jacketed brigade captains with petrol torches melted into the thicket. The sun rose like a scarlet moon. The ground was black, the air was hot and a few ancient stumps blazed near the front door. The heavy machines and their minders moved on, but fire stalked the house from all directions.

Over the next four days, side by side with a succession of local mates, I battled renegade blazes with wet sacks, shovels and a chainsaw. I grew fond of my tea-towel and catnapped in my boots. When winds gusted, Victorian tankers and their beefy crew arrived to stop the 'spotting', a term I hadn't heard since birth classes. Another worry was 'crowning' (flames soaring through tree tops), a word which also recalled the drama of parturition.

When the last tankers left, myself and a sequence of 'buddies' resumed hand-to-hand combat, as army helicopters criss-crossed the sky and flare-ups persisted. This was the fire that wouldn't go away. There was no time to answer the phone, wash our faces or rustle up a quiche. I barely slept for a week, and never felt better. All of us felt the same, even the ones who had attended classes in breast-feeding. None of us had seen a woman for . . . oh, months . . . and managed to refrain from expressing our sense of loss. A firefighter later reported his wife had shaved her legs, put on a dress and begged him not to wash off the soot. Then came the mopping-up, more fun than mopping. A neighbour, an apron-clad wimp who hosts the local playgroup, pleaded: 'Let's start our own fire brigade.' Us blokes scratched our designs for a scarf in the smouldering soil with flaming sticks.

When the Missus finally made it home, I was sprawled on the parquetry gnawing charred kangaroo tail, wearing nothing but a Lone Ranger tea-towel. 'Chuck me a beer,' I snarled, burping. That was two weeks ago, and she is still under sedation.

(*The Guardian*)

36

The Worth of the Wild

At a time when the bush was briefly held in disrepute because of the fires, I was asked to celebrate its virtues. Easy. A place where wild things happen . . . plus lots of sex and slugs and rocks.

1994:

The entire focus of the baby boomers from the moment they left school until the dawning of the age of ecology was on the city. It was where the wild things were – drag queens, drugs, parties and twenty-four-hour hamburgers. You could meet brooding poet/gangsters in jazz cafés, or see them breeding in foreign movies. Cappuccino-inflamed words bubbled into the wee small hours: anarchy, acid, anal intercourse, Janis Joplin, Cuba. Missing from this list, you will notice, are nature, environment, fauna, abseiling, khaki walk shorts and the National Park.

Wilderness was never mentioned, though we all yearned to be wild, like Marlon Brando and Oscar. A tree was something you bumped into when pissed. The first ever Oz rock song was entitled, 'I'm a Wild One' ('gonna break loose . . .'). This meant visiting King's Cross and ordering raisin toast. Until 1977, not a single Sydneyside under forty had ever travelled west of Parramatta. The 'mountains' meant chilblains, hot water bottles, a vista of Victorian rest homes. At least we were greener than our counterparts in London or New York, being dimly aware of one natural phenomenon, the surf, though it was less a matter of hanging

five than hanging out at Surf City, the disco. Landscape was
booooring.

And then my mother acquired a cliff-edge weekender. Wispy
overgrown trails led to places with storybook names, like Fairy
Glenn and Bushrangers Cave, where you could roam for hours
in surprising solitude. Or with your girlfriend. Despite the
bushflies, making love on a mossy slab in the Grose Valley,
with testicles dangling quaintly in the chilly rapids near Junction
Rock, was better than a backseat quickie at the Drive-in, so long
as you were on top. Nature in the raw.

Even so, for the next twenty-five years I forgot all about the
outdoors; so busy was I scouring the city nightscape for a hot
dance floor. Not once, not even in America, with its stretches
of spectacular remoteness and a mythology of beatniks hunting
dharma in the Rockies, did I ever contemplate shopping for
hiking boots. The closest I came to a shrub was in Central
Park, trying to score a joint.

Back home in the seventies, the bush was still unfashionable.
Trails were deserted, few were signposted. One afternoon I
found a track called Porter's Pass, not far from the Blackheath
Post Office. It skipped across glens, snaked through caves,
descended a sheer cliff beside a swirling waterfall and opened
to a ledge overlooking Megalong Valley. Who was this person
called Porter, I wondered, teasing this leafy filament from the
surly escarpment, and bequeathing it to the nation? All of the
local trails, I later discovered, were experiential works of art –
created by nature and crafted by gifted bushies. Just as Rodin
liberated his immortal subjects lurking in the blocks of marble,
so Porter, Govet, Neate, Rodriguez and all the rest uncovered
the hidden treasures of the wild and presented them to future
hordes of backpackers.

There is danger in wilderness. Climbers crash, Boy Scouts
lose their way, tourists trip over their tripods. It's a metaphor
of the unconscious; dark, mysterious, threatening. Hence the
call of the wild can be drowned by the shriek of suburbia – make

it safe. Build toilets, fire trails, fencing, a kiosk . . . The concept of wilderness is dismissed as 'philosophically repugnant'. Fires become an excuse to tame the interior, to scorch a black line, to turn the Grose Valley into a drag strip for Jeeps.

The National Park in flames is a frightening sight; a tree once hugged now burns with desire to consume your house. But the current push to subdue the bush is even more frightening. Danger is elemental. Who would climb Mt Everest, if it was ringed with a safety net? A tamed wilderness is a neutered nation.

During the January inferno, thousands of everyday people displayed qualities they didn't even know they possessed. Life became more demanding than television, and more revealing. My smalltown grocer seemed just another bloated yob, until I saw him facing a sheet of flame with a tea-towel around his mouth. Since the 'disaster', our community is healthier and wiser, so much so that one resident remarked: 'There are not enough crises in our life.' As a resource, the value of wilderness is beyond measure, which confuses the economists and politicians. It is the last unknown – only by plunging into it can we know ourselves. And by learning to live with wilderness, danger and all, we can better learn to live with each other.

(*Out There*)

37
Hard Target, Soft Touch

From Fidel Castro to Jean Claude van Damme, from Greenpeace to the Ceiling Doctor . . . In Surfers' Paradise, a journey of a thousand lifetimes only takes you as far as the Travel Lodge buffet – but can you empty your plate in ninety minutes?

1994:

The future is a difficult place to find, though I have been to Surfers' Paradise. It was less vile than expected. To stroll a shopping centre full of Japanese signs is relaxing, especially when the merchandise is unenticing and the touts discourage all but Asian honeymooners. Rumours are rife. I was assured that the jeweller at one super-chic mall had sold a watch to a tourist for 2 million dollars. Anything is possible in this Zen-like fantasy town, with its soaring apartments lining the beach.

It makes you swim early in the day, before the shade hits the sand, allowing more time for lunch. Here, the buffet is king. Gluttony is a fad. When I arrived at the revolving restaurant, eager to dip my own snout in the trough, the maître d' offered his commiserations: 'you don' really have enough time. We'll be clearing the buffet in an hour and a half.'

Next stop was the casino. Vast, glittery, throbbing – yet everyone looking sad. I don't get it with these joints, fast sprouting across the West, but it's the future. For those prone to shopping withdrawal during blackjack, a monorail zooms across the road to the mall. For those prone to gambling withdrawal at coffee-breaks, the Keno cards are stacked near the sugar box. A big thank-you to Japan, incidentally, for Keno and Karaoke.

What I liked about being in Surfers' for a day is that it forced me to play against type. To be someone else for a change. On the Travelodge console, the in-house videos were spectacularly violent, so I crushed the sensitive New Age sap within, and sampled the wares of Jean Claude Van Damme. Oh my. The violence was so excessively cartoonic as to be bland, and the politics endearingly radical. It made me a soft touch for *Hard Target*. In this movie, massive wealth is equated with murderous intent. Van Damme is no James Bond, serving the State; he is a Fidel Castro thrusting up from Skid Row, mauling the richees. Feel-good splatterpunk. An oxy-moron, of course, like Surfers' Paradise.

OK, so why was I there? To give the opening address at a national convention of franchisors, on consumer trends. Ironic, really, seeing that I distrust the standardization of experience that flows in the wake of franchise-mania. Yet the system gives battlers a chance to better their future, perhaps, and to slip from the grind of the boss or the dole. A snowballing franchise with a feel-good agenda can be an agent of change.

Donut King puts a contact number on its containers for parents and kids in crisis. Pastor Reynolds, who runs Close to the Edge Missions, says that as a result of calls received via Donut King, he has personally counselled young people back from the brink of suicide.

Over twenty years ago, one of the first ships chartered by Greenpeace sailed into Vancouver Harbour to stop the slaughter of whales. On board was a teenager, Kaaydah Schatten, a founder member. Where is she now? In Dallas running an international franchise with a turnover of 10 million dollars. She still pursues her Greenpeace goals, but in a way which is unglamorous, effective and aimed at protecting the health of office workers.

Ms Schatten's outfit is Ceiling Doctor. 150 million work days are lost every year in the UK due to respiratory problems. Offices are hothouses of dust, pollen, bacteria, smoke, mould and other disease-causing contaminants. Ceiling Doctor restores sick buildings, at a fraction of the costs of repainting or replacement. 'These days I'm not just communicating an environmental message,' she says, 'but doing something positive about it.'

After my immersion in the world of franchising, gazing in savage self-absorbtion from a Travelodge window at the logo-rimmed Pacific highway, I began to think about branding my own franchise. If only I hadn't squandered my youth being caught up in concepts, instead of consumer goods, I could have been the Colonel Sanders of the counter-culture. Yes, my cosmeticized face on every mall, a heli-pad in every tax haven. The product? Foodaceuticals, a hot trend.

Functional foods are the new frontier. Think of calcium-fortified fruit juices and breakfast cereal with betacarotene, fibre, Niacin and Riboflarin, devised to turn us into gold medal Olympians. In the future, foodaceuticals, or pharmafoodicals, will blend smart drugs with organic ingredients and deep sea plankton to enhance IQ, athletic performance or sexual desire. Maybe all three at once. Plus, delay ageing. Then we can join MENSA, move to Hollywood and live forever.

Some of these smart drugs are on the shelves, boringly packaged, legal and apparently safe. The next step is to mix them with an exotic soya bean thick-shake, add the ingredient of fun, shout it from the rooftops and send me a commission. Dancing boys on the counter, Dick's dial on the logo, planetary health as the goal, millionaire me the result. It's strange what Surfers' Paradise does to the brain. Next Father's Day, I'll be wanting a billion-dollar watch.

(*Australian Business Monthly*)

38
Frocks, Chainsaws and the Emperor Aurelius

Blundering about in the ethical jungle with hip-hop academics.

1996:

However infuriating for authors and booksellers, because of the minuscule mark-ups, the Penguin 60s mini-books have conquered the world. The hit treat of this literary smorgasbord, ranging from splatterpunk grunge to dotty fairytales, is a surprise – the meditations of a Roman emperor never portrayed by Charlton Heston.

'Observe how transient and trivial is all mortal life,' wrote Marcus Aurelius eighteen centuries ago, 'yesterday a drop of semen, tomorrow a handful of spice.' His own transience is now in doubt, having been resurrected as a hot property. What accounts for the triumph of his *Meditations*? No scandal or gossip is attached to them, no marketing machine has singled him out.

'Always think of the universe as one living organism,' advises Aurelius, 'with a single substance and a single soul.' His thoughts are clear, honourable, and wise. They reflect a coherent worldview; the gods are respected, cynicism is lacking. Perhaps his books fly out the door because his thoughts fly in face of pop-think. Here at last – an emperor with clothes.

To maintain a bedrock of core beliefs is difficult in this uncertain age. It is an area in which I sense a split between post-mod academics and the business community. One group clings to the canon, the other tries to blow it away.

To guide executives through the gauntlet of modern moral dilemmas, crash courses are springing up in ethics, political philosophy and the Great Books. Lodwrick Cook, then CEO of oil giant Atlantic Ritchfield, was 'frankly, skeptical that immersion in the Great Ideas would be of immediate value' in honing his grip on the tiller, but after attending a seminar in Aspen, he 'learned otherwise'. Cook emerged with a Values Compass, 'a framework for the executive to create order out of the growing chaos of cultural diversity and conflict of values'.

Aristotle apparently conceived of 'something quite like' the futures market, Kant supported free market economics, and Locke's theory of property reveals why capital gains are 'in fact earned as legitimately as salaries and wages'. Mmmmmm.

There is something heartening about top execs marching off to quell the complexities of ethics, minority rights and ecological woes, armed with a Masters of Business Administration, the Great Books, and a Values Compass.

Hip-hop academics, on the other hand, are blundering about in a semiotic swamp. During my damp Christmas in a forested cottage, a pride of feminists quaffing champagne thrilled to the delights of the hottest femporn, as I was hunched over suds in the sink. One cutting edge tract depicts dildonic activity in the vegetable aisle of a supermarket. As the enthusiasm of my bright friends mounted for the work, along with the intake of alcohol, I bleated through the burnt saucepans: 'What's so great about it?' The prose style, perhaps; or a fab take on the meaning of life? The answer landed with a familiar thud.

In unison: 'It's subversive!' Cheers.

The ring of the word has lost none of its lustre. A delicious frisson of James Dean, Rosa Luxemburg and the Simpsons. Kill the patriarchy. Subvert the dominant paradigm. Say fuck at a funeral. Mopping the champers off the cushions, I am wondering how many orthodoxies still need to be subverted, apart from the consumer society.

Gushing over a text because its vulgarity is a welcome affront to straight society is also subversive – of free-thinking. That game has been won. These days there is such pluralism of style, opinions and subcultures that subversion for its own sake is reactionary . . . a rip-off rebellion of colour and movement and photo-opportunities which plays into the hands of crass marketing. In today's soaring tumult, the opposite impulse is required – to enchant an audience with a life-affirming vision and a moral core that goes beyond shopping and brushing up on aqua-aerobics.

The non-bookish lesbian community on the edge of town pursues its dreams with approval and respect from the lads at the pub. Driving trucks, sinking mighty poles, these muscular bundles of oestrogen mount and maintain the biggest tractors, and swing the heaviest brands of chainsaws. Having formed their own fire brigade, they recently assembled to hear an advisory address. 'I won't begin with my usual warnings to women who face the prospect of fighting a fire,' said the gritty local commander, 'that frocks are not a good idea. I can see that such a warning isn't necessary.'

The tyranny of conformity has long been overthrown, and smart business is alert to the colourful world of optional lifestyles. Rural lesbians are a booming market for tractor parts, chainsaw lubricants and roomy overalls. Phallus fruit is fast bucks in the city, but in 2,000 years will it still be ripe? Our time is but a moment, reminds Marcus Aurelius. Yesterday a drop of semen, tomorrow a rotten zucchini.

(*The Bulletin*)

39
The Bonfire on the Lake

For a special issue of The Bulletin *on the meaning of Australia Day.*

1996:

Some of the best minds born in Australia live on the other side of the world. Their bitter homeland portraits are widely syndicated. One summer, wondering if they knew something I didn't, I gathered a collection of their outpourings and took them on a family holiday, planning to read them.

Jamming the children, their friends and their mother into a station wagon packed to the roof-rack, I drove several hours to a place which, by a curious twist of the highway, had not yet been 'discovered' and turned into the Mighty Marlin theme park.

The mud brick house stood in 100 acres of spotted gum forest, backed by the Pacific Ocean and overlooking a bird-covered lake. As we unloaded the bags, including a laundry basket stacked with expatriate essays on the horrors of Ockerdom, seven feet of yellow-and-black Diamond Python slithered in a relaxed and friendly fashion across the verandah. Our family walked the sandy track to the beach. Serene, vast, unoccupied; the dolphins rode the breakers, driftwood lay tangled among yellow flowers in the dunes. 'Spaciousness' is a word repeated on meditation tapes as a desirable state, ever elusive; in this land it is a gift, which more and more Australians are utilizing.

Four-wheel-drives lurch up the adjacent mountain, driven by Aboriginal elders, who introduce visitors into the basics of songlines, bush-tucker and the Dreamtime. On the edge of our beach, waves surged through a channel into a lake, creating hydrotherapy pools. As the tide dropped, I took a plastic bucket and swam to the rocks, from which the saucer-sized mussels were easy to pluck. That night we sat under the gums steaming the shellfish with fresh coriander and wine in an iron pot and tossing titbits to the possums.

The next morning I sorted through the photocopied opinions of Pilger, Greer, Humphries and James, in preparation to better understand my country, when an old codger – briefly met at the general store – pulled up in his pick-up.

'Like I promised,' he said, 'as many as you can carry.'

Warily, I wanted to know what gear was required. Sure, I like oysters, but I dreaded an arduous day of prizing them off barnacled rocks with a chisel. And I had reading to do.

'Old sneakers and a bucket,' he said.

Ten minutes later, we were sloshing the upstream banks of the lake, flipping oysters off the mud by the score, observed by a flotilla of black swans.

Back in the kitchen, I tipped a mountain on to the table. 'But they're not open,' complained the Missus, having never seen an oyster outside a restaurant. 'No worries,' said the codger. 'Two minutes max in the microwave, and they grin atcha.'

Aussie champagne washed down our three dozen each in the filtered sunlight and bushflower-scented air, as the children chased a goanna away from the ducks. After an afternoon surf, more Tarzan-like gathering of shellfish under a purple sky and yet another feast of nature's bounty, I settled on the couch for a late-night browse of the Oz-excoriating polemic. At that moment, urgent shouts echoed from the lake, so I decided to investigate. Wallabies thumped through the forest as I groped along the track to the bridge.

Nation states are faced with obsolescence as we are thrust towards globalization, and the process of 'defining our identity'

has the ring of a lost era, of vaudeville, and the Boer War. Yet much to my surprise, since resettling here in 1980, the special qualities of the place have dented my satirical armour. A turning point was the 1985 handback of Uluru and its surrounds to the original owners, a ceremony at which I experienced the novel sensation of national pride. Later, when Prime Minister Paul Keating made his speech at Redfern, apologizing to Aborigines for past injustices, it seemed possible that reconciliation could be achieved this century. The ultimate step will be an indigenous pardon.

In a nutshell, it is the exalted revelation that all things are possible which singles Australia out. The problems are immense, but at least they don't date back to the crusades or a potato famine, or involve topical horrors like ethnic cleansing. We are young, vigorous, inventive.

Despite the adolescent aberrations of our character, from the tall poppy syndrome to the worship of sport and our abasement at the juggernaut of McCulture, the future looks fascinating. And not just because of the Republic, with its languid inevitability. It's like trying to whip yourself into a frenzy over the law of gravity.

More intriguing is the paradox of our Asianization, taken to a new dimension with the Djakarta 'agreement'. However many samosas sizzle in woks at school fêtes, or holidays notched up in Bali, the lifestyle of our land is wayward and unique. We should be wary of calls from Singapore and Tokyo to tighten our belts, buckle down, get on with the job. I once boarded a Japanese tour bus at a Sydney hotel, along with an English interpreter. As it chugged through the rush hour, the guide at the mike drew attention to the pedestrians thronging to the office. 'See how slowly they walk,' she said. 'What a lazy country.' Personally, I like the way we walk.

If we can hang on to this pace a little longer, it will reap rewards. Burnt-out execs from Asia and America may yet be sent to these shores to learn how to slow down, to relax, to become psychically retooled. The tourist industry could be transformed, as futurist Peter Ellyard has pointed out, into the wellbeing industry, where skilled bushies use the cosmic landscape to reinvigorate the over-stretched.

What we already possess, if left alone, appreciates. Sixty years ago, an orchardist descended a trail in the Blue Mountains with a stack of seedlings. As his team sharpened their axes and saws, in preparation for the felling of Blue Gum Forest, a party of bushwalkers happened by. Horrified at the impending walnut plantation, they persuaded the orchardist to hold off, until funds could be found to buy him out. In the ensuing brouhaha, the Blue Mountains National Park was gazetted, and the forest saved. This wilderness has since out-earned the projected revenue of walnuts a million times over.

The water under the bridge glistened with pinpricks of light, as though reflecting the stars, and voices in alien dialects and shrieks of children hung in the air. Swish, splash; swish, splash. Leaning over the rails, I deciphered a scene of family groups, including Aborigines and Asians, wading the shallows with torches held underwater, tipping the wriggling prawns from nets into tubs. As yet, you don't need to be rich in Oz, to live rich.

And so the days on the coast rolled by. The road snaked through national parks, where, in a string of beaches and tidal lakes, a thousand busy species vanished from suburban beaches presented an alternative to art galleries.

From a headland, we watched a whale the size of a church roll around and squirt the sky. A local identity had been fined for riding on the back of a whale, dividing the town. He had meant no harm. Whale Dundee had wanted to frolic in its watery ambit, and claims he found himself unexpectedly born aloft when the mammal surfaced. Yahooo . . . ride 'em, cowboy. Listening to the portside fishermen discuss the evolution of eco-etiquette, with their laconic tolerance and wit, I was reminded of characters out of Henry Lawson and of the national predilection to take the piss, as well as to drink it.

Despite the suffocating prevalence of suburbia, the hinterlands are full of alternatives. Backyard inventors in solar-powered redoubts creating efficient tigerworm toilets, forest ferals in tepees downloading recipes for ecstasy from the FBI. From this compost sprouts a rich, tantalizing culture of music and theatre, dance and mime, festivals and mystic rituals.

The absence of an ingrained caste or class is another plus. When playing host to friends from England, I am constantly surprised by the continuing grip on the conversation of social-demarcations. From the tweak of a diphthong, the pom is quick to ascertain a countryman's place of birth, class and educational institutions attended. Our equivalent to class is cars.

London is full of professors and doctors in rust-buckets. Here, as we intensify our embrace of materialism, at least in the mainstream, the appurtenances of wealth deepen as status symbols. My clapped-out Holden is acceptable in the scrubs, but mingling with fatcats in the city, their air of disdain, verging on shock, is palpable.

Foreigners all profess to love Oz, of course, but it's only Le Tan deep. As soon as the deluge starts, they make you feel responsible. You try to interest them in the multi-hued pastels of the wet eucalypt bark, but they dash off to Queensland and the Reef, and, so frequently, to further implacable torrents.

The sky was clear, however, on our last night of vacation and the moon was full. The kids heaved the sunbleached logs into a pile on the flat sandy banks of the lake, as neighbours disgorged iceboxes and picnic baskets. The chit-chat centred on the conflict between laidback lifestyle and in-depth culture. I recalled my last dinner party in London, where a short-listed Booker author dismissed the entire output of my compatriots:

'You Aussies are too affable,' he said, 'and too free of crises to create anything of worth.' Wisdom could only be gleaned from the slopes of Vesuvius. 'That's why I choose to live in a flat in Clapham,' he thundered, though his wife whispered in my ear that the prodigy spent most of his time at a weekender in Cornwall.

In the mauve dusk of the beach the champagne popped, the tower of driftwood burst into flames, and I was curious to know how the children managed to get it alight, with such a drastic shortage of litter. Others joined the circle, grilling their abalone and prawns. I decided to grill my daughter. 'It was easy, Dad. That pile of paper you've been carting around all week . . .' The laundry basket, bereft of its brooding bundle of photocopies, lay by the edge of the roaring fire, its wisdom unheeded.

But Ah my foes, and Oh my friends, it gave a lovely light.

(The Bulletin)

40
Joan of Arc in a Lear Jet

Corporate success in rewarded with stretch limos, million dollar share options and country weekends with prime ministers. Do-gooders in non-profit agencies and the faceless executives who throw lifebuoys to underdogs are rarely the Biz Page pin-ups. Perhaps it's just as well. The lack of distraction lets them get on with saving lives.

1996:

A year after leaving her small-town high school, Hayley Beavis was still out of a job. She was morose and insecure. Every time she applied for work her hopes rallied, only to crash with each rejection. Like millions of youths the world over, she felt stuck in dole ghetto. The morning she put on her best black jeans and turned up at a local fabric store for a job interview, Hayley felt like a loser. 'I didn't present well,' she recalls. A future in retailing was an unlikely option for this teenager from Warrnambool, Australia who had a phobia of cash-registers.

To her surprise, she was accepted for a year's trial. On one condition – that she undergo an intensive, six-week pre-employment programme with Breaking the Cycle, a youth-reach agency. 'We are not about providing welfare,' insists its general manager, 'we're about changing people's lives'. It sounded like rhetoric from my day, only this time the nuts and bolts were in place.

The 'non-sporty' Hayley Beavis found herself lugging a hefty backpack on a gruelling trek, along with thirty youngsters considered 'at risk' – runaways, the homeless, petty crims and even plump, secure kids with loving parents who felt shut out of the job market. The trek was followed by a fifty-mile bicycle safari, a canoe trip and, after moving into crowded dormitories with a bunch of strangers, training in 'lifeskills'.

'It's about what it means to be human,' says John Tripodi of Break the Cycle, referring to an arsenal of processes aimed at 'altering the behaviour which stops them achieving what they want. We provide a safe place to tell the truth, – a stew of new age psychotherapy blended with age-old self-esteem mantras. Hayley remembers: 'It was hell.' Her two weeks in the dorm felt like six months. 'But I learnt how to spill my guts.' The teenager emerged with a new found sense of reliance, a belief that the future was hers to mould.

Breaking the Cycle is government-funded, which makes me feel fine about paying taxes, but driven by business. Over 500 teenagers have completed the course ('There are no drop-outs,' assures Tripodi). Six months later, eighty-five per cent of graduates remain in full-time employment. Eighteen months after the course, Hayley Beavis was appointed manager of the haberdashery department in her hometown branch of Spotlight, the country's largest textile retailer, where the cash register never stops tinkling.

'There are many wins for us,' says the chain's operations manager, Linda Mira-Bateman, 'although some people are cynical. They see it as a way of getting people on the floor cheap. Others reckon we're taking on duds.' In fact, Spotlight's stores have been infused with a range of life skills and staff morale has soared. 'These recruits are real goers,' Mira-Bateman breezes, 'it's given everyone a strong sense of caring.' Spotlight's own team leaders have acquired additional skills, and 'it's even led us to update our training programmes'. Such is her firm's enthusiasm, their suppliers are now being pushed to be part of Breaking the Cycle.

As the Social Responsibility movement gathers pace and

widens its spectrum – local communities, ethics, the environment, Brazilian tribes – so too, the critics sharpen their swords. Its familiar icons, such as The Body Shop's Anita Roddick, are caricatured as touchy-feely loonies who've 'mesmerized' their boards as they swagger across the globe 'doing good' with imperious autocracy, like Joan of Arc in a Lear jet.

So that's a crime?

'There is only one social responsibility of business,' the economist Milton Friedman huffed and puffed back in the sixties. 'To use its resources and engage in activities designed to increase profits . . .' This is less convincing now than it ever was. The monetary might of the multinationals has, put them in the driving seat of many Third World economies. Either they use this power responsibly, and focus on issues of social justice, or they sow the seeds of future insurrection. Besides, doing good is good for business.

The United Parcel Service in the US established a programme for its managers back in 1968, partly in response to the Civil Rights Act. Run by non-profit agencies in every community, it sends teams to work in homeless shelters, food kitchens and drug centres. Invariably, the experience is life-changing for its staff, who are 'less quick to judge others and take more time to talk to people different from themselves.'

A New York survey of nearly 500 corporations involved in volunteer schemes found staff skills were enhanced in areas of time management, communications, innovation, risk-taking, stress control, survival, priority setting and resistance to feelings of isolation and alienation. Community programmes boost staff motivation, productivity and thus corporate performance.

Shortly before his untimely death, the head of Esprit Australia, John Bell, put forward the case for a corporate conscience. 'Business must stand for more than making a profit,' he said. 'There are two great benefits in doing this: the best people will want to work for you and the consumers will want to support you. Be informed, be involved – make a difference.' Bell preferred to invest in social programmes – such as teaching 'misfits' the techniques of organic market gardening – than to place an ad in *Vogue*.

It has been pointed out that true leaders do more than embrace change. They hunt out ways to transform their organization for the better. And in so doing, they transform the environment in which we live . . . not to mention the lives of people like Hayley Beavis.

(*The Bulletin*)

41
Millennial Fever

The future leaves its footprints on the sand, but a lot of people are afraid to look – especially politicians. Election campaigns invariably raise 'the vision thing', and the response is a merry-go-round of bewilderment, platitudes and chauvinist cheerleading. Herewith gleanings from the wonderful world of 'deep futurism'.

1996:

These brain triggers are drawn from disparate sources, respectable and otherwise. Lest you're inclined to dismiss them as 'airy fairy imaginings', we'll start with an anecdote told at a seminar designed to create 'global scenarios' for the 21st century:

A consultant from the management firm McKinsey was sent to Japan to work with a multimedia multinational. The brief was to create a vision plan for the next thirty years. On his first day, the consultant was asked by the president to consider where the company would be in a thousand years time. 'That's far too far ahead,' gasped the man from McKinsey. No, to clarify this goal would be helpful, insisted the president, so they could work back to the year 2025. It was finally decided that in the year 3000 the company would market a musical instrument which sang directly to the human soul.

Okay? So having a bash at the next twenty years should be a pushover.

@A key cabinet post for the next millennium will be the Minister for Consequences. His brief will be to prepare scenarios on the long-term impact of new policies. The consequence of this is unpredictable.

@Champagne and caviar are yesterday's luxuries. Tomorrow's is time.

@The disappearance of time means that the shelf-life of management knowledge is down to two years, and shrinking. So . . .

@The only basis of competitive advantage among firms will be the ability to learn faster than anyone else and then to act on that learning.

@OUTMODED ETHICS OF BUSINESS: Competitors are the enemy; the game is to win; life is a jungle.

@NEW ETHICS OF BUSINESS: Competitors are my benchmark; the game is perpetual development; the world is my community.

@Two hundred years ago, shoppers had access to less than 300 products. Today we can choose from over a million. Now what?

@Most adults can recognize over a thousand brand names, and can't name five locally-growing plants. Will our survival depend on reversing this ratio?

@An hour of judicious downloading from the internet will put more data at your fingertips than was absorbed in a lifetime in Beethoven's day – but what use are facts you can't act upon?

@The array of technical knowledge at our disposal today

represents about one per cent of the knowledge that will be available in fifty years time.

The sea level is rising ten times faster than it was fifty years ago.

The imperialists of old, with their glass beads and trinkets, sailed the oceans backed by the flag. Now, traders surf the internet with digital cargo – the imperialism of knowledge. The compu-nerds of today will be the power-brokers of tomorrow.

The Web warps gender. Mr CyberSnag is deeply sensitive, vulnerable and open to 'feminine emotional swings'. The CyberSheila is tough and intellectually empowered; she is independent, non-passive and defies the label of 'oppressed luddite babe'.

The lunge into cyberspace will be matched by a plunge into inner space – meditation, dreamwork, holistic therapies and vision-conjuring.

Since World War II, the rate of depressive illness in Western societies has increased tenfold. In the future, sunlight will be used to treat depression.

DOWNTRENDS: Dry-cleaning; duck-hunts; Ferraris.

UPTRENDS: Aromatherapy; solo sex; voluntary simplicity.

There's no avant garde any more, because there's no cultural élite trying to preserve order and tradition.

The sweeping away of traditional values and lifestyles puts a mental strain on millions of people. This will either transform our capacities and prompt an evolution of human psychology, or it will trigger a global psychotic collapse.

◉ The workplace of the future will need to foster psycho-spiritual growth, or suffer rapid stuff turnover.

◉ Today's marginal dollar is spent on entertainment peripherals such as videos, CDs and software. Tomorrow, it will be spent on tools for spiritual growth.

◉ Brain-mind technologies will be harnessed to influence our emotions, sensations, memory, learning capacity and other psychological states. The Walkman 2000 will feature a conscience meter, and will be called the Dalai Lama-man.

◉ In the olden days, the ego-centre was the heart. Now it's the brain. The future seat of the self could be projected into cyberspace, attaching itself to virtual bodies. This could enable us to see the world through another's eyes and enlarge our frontiers of compassion.

◉ Virtual reality is the tangible replication of a world that has been with us all our lives – in our imagination, literature and dreams – but it costs a bomb.

◉ Expanding Islam versus the global civilization of the West is shaping up for a shoot-out. One system is based on a secular materialism, the other on faith; one has rejected belief altogether, the other has placed it at the centre of its world-view.

◉ The primal religious myth needed in the future will not be divisive, nor confined to a privileged society in a bounded field. It will speak to the world for all people, all life. The first planetary myth.

@ Reports of bizarre encounters with UFOs will escalate, as will the credibility of witnesses. The question of whether or not UFOs are 'real' will be overshadowed by speculations on the *significance* of the sightings. Could UFOs be a cry from the collective unconscious, a plea for magic in a materialistic age? Or the first tremors of cosmic hallucination, designed to lure us from earth – the cradle of humankind – out into the twinkling nightscape.

@ Fifty years ago we could identify two galaxies. Now we can identify two billion galaxies.

@ Health-conscious boomers will extend the most expensive years of their lives on a fixed income. Cooking at home will catch on. The sewing basket will return to the hearth. Past extravagancies will be recalled with wistful bemusement.

@ BOOMERS VERSUS BUSTERS: Our war: Vietnam (bad); their war: Desert Storm (good). Our toy: the frisbee; their toy: Nintendo. Our majors: literature, psychology, sociology; their majors: business, computers, women's studies. Our terror: getting old; their terror: looking after us.

@ FADING FORCES: Shareholders; Boy Scouts; atheists.

@ RISING FORCES: Stakeholders; backpackers; Jungians.

@ The data stored in our brain as units of memory could be transferred to a computer and downloaded to another brain, extending our life beyond bodily death.

@ The birth of the millennium will see the decline of youth culture. (And not before time. Hurrumph!)

@ In 2025, national service may well be compulsory. Young

people will be given the option to work with the poor or disabled, to repair the environment, or to take their skills to a distant, impoverished land.

Second and third careers will become the norm; so much so, that they will no longer be preceded by a mid-life crisis.

IDEAS IN DECLINE: Nation states; treating the world as a quarry; technology in neutral; growth is good; spank to punish.

IDEAS ON THE RISE: Community; everything is connected; corporate conscience; the worth of the wild; spank to please.

The growth of genetics will lead to programmes that enhance the physical and mental abilities . . . of the rich.

Breakthroughs in genetics mean we are starting to redesign our own species, blurring the ancient boundaries of our coming to life and the leaving of it.

It is predicted that some people alive today will still be alive in 400 years. That's a lot of shopping.

More and more of us could become composite beings – part biological, part mechanical, part electronic. We will adjust our own brains to boost IQ, filter pain and intensify pleasure. As a super-élite of cyborgs, we could end up ruling the world – or be rounded up and dismantled.

The fastest growing branch of medicine is plastic surgery.

Digitized voice replication will convey a faultless reproduction of how we sound. It will shatter our sense of identity and further disrupt the meaning of 'authentic'. Elvis sightings are a portent. The King will return to the charts with new material, appear on MTV and promote whisky.

◉ Now that history and fantasy can be blended with seamless conviction, where does it leave the concept of reality?

◉ DOWN TRENDS: The manicured lawn; heaven up top; feed-the-kids-pork.

◉ UP TRENDS: Herb lawns; heaven within; feed-the-kids-lentils.

◉ Within twenty years, nearly three quarters of the world's population will be urbanized.

◉ Most of the industrialized world will soon run out of convenient space for landfills.

◉ Prepare for global management. The macro-engineers are waiting in the wings, ready to manipulate the oceans, forests, grasslands and water supplies of the world.

◉ Extraction of raw materials through mining, logging and drilling will fade away, to be replaced by resource recovery through recycling, reclamation and remanufacturing.

◉ In the future, food crops will not be exposed to weather, disease, insects or pollution because they will be raised in climate-controlled factories. These can be located anywhere – desert, mountain, city or slum. Farmers will work indoors and wear hemp suits.

◉ MacDonald's fodder: a person unaware of the connection between food and the landscape; a passive consumer; an Industrial Eater.

@IN DECLINE: Scientific objectivity; a fixed address; the primacy of print; the GNP as a barometer of national health; motorways; three meals-a-day.

@ON THE RISE: The feminization of leadership; bicycles; snacking; eco-economics; easy-fit jeans.

@ Humanity is gearing up for the party of a lifetime – New Year's Eve, 1999; a new decade, a new century, a new era. The first children to be educated entirely in the third millennium are already born; the houses and cars of 2001 are already designed. Party-goers will look back a thousand years to the highs, the lows, and they will look ahead to the next thousand. The Rolling Stones have been booked for the night, poor things, by which time they might have found satisfaction. After the morning hangover, the task ahead will be amazing – to re-invent the conditions of a civilized life for a new period of history.

See you there.

(Sources: *Cyberspace, The Futurist Magazine*, assorted conferences)

42
Rupert in Ecotopia

The rapid rise of Rupert Murdoch, and his effect on planetary culture, is usually greeted with acclaim. The tycoon is seen as a visionary, an electronic equivalent to Alexander the Great. Other visionaries – the ones without inordinate wealth and a media empire – must rely on the power of their ideas to reach a mass audience. In the future, what if opposing champions met face-to-face, as they once did in ancient Athens?

335BC/2013:

Alex, the most powerful man in the world, asked to be taken to meet a homeless derelict, nicknamed the Dog, found sprawled on the steps of the Parthenon. Towering over him, the General asked: 'Is there anything I can do for you?'

'There is,' snapped the beggar. 'Stand out of my sun.'

The General retreated, remarking to his companions, 'If I was not Alexander the Great, then I would be Diogenes, the Dog.'

Diogenes, the famous Cynic, dressed in rags and slept in a clay pot. In reaction to an age of vulgarity and love of wealth, his teachings stressed voluntary simplicity, and were conveyed by personal example. Sold as a slave, he scolded the powerful (including Plato, a 'sell-out') and regarded himself the one free man in Athens.

It is recorded that these two men – the one who had everything and the one who had nothing – died on the same day.

A latter-day equivalent of this encounter took place between Rupert the Mighty, at his Los Angeles studios, and a tribal elder from Ecotopia, a settlement in the heart of Mabo Country, in Australia's tropical north. The year is 2013. The magnate initiated the meeting, his face appearing on screen from the tree-side monitor. 'Is there anything I can do for you, chief?'

The Elder glanced at the image – splat! – his well-aimed gob of chewed Yukkaberry dribbled down the screen. 'Sure – you can stamp out the *Sun*.'

'Let's be reasonable,' Rupert soothed . . .

'And cut all the crap you broadcast.'

'If I did, the mass audience wouldn't hear of your mind-stretching lifestyle, your wonder . . .'

'Around here, Rupe, ratings don't mean a thing.' If the elders in Ecotopia courted popularity, they were distrusted. (Echoing a dictum of Diogenes. 'What's the use of a philosophy that doesn't hurt people's feelings?') A flunkey from Global Megopolis sponged the spittle off the screen, revealing that Rupert hadn't aged a day since the nineties, thanks to laser cosmetics. The Elder resumed his yogic Pose of Tranquillity, clad in a G-string of fig leaves. A camcorder shot the images back to LA. This meeting mattered to Rupert, because of his empire's dependence on growth and the lure of an untapped market, but the presumption of the Elder got on his goat: 'According to my academic advisers you're just a knucklehead trying to be a philosopher.'

The Elder laughed. 'Yes, that's what a philosopher is.'

'Just because you and your friends occupy the last rainforests on earth doesn't give you the right to shut out the media.' These days, in the 'shopping-mall' nations of Asia and Eastern Europe, pay TV was pumped into every dwelling, by law.

The Ecotopians had held their ground. Mabo Country stretched from the woody outskirts of Byron Bay to Cape York, skirting the sad slum strip of Surfers-to-Noosa, and absorbed vast areas of hinterland. The eco-principality was

managed by Kooris, in unison with greenies, forest ferals and
neo cyber-punks, the high-tech whizz-kids of self-sustainability.
It was all 'off the grid' (some said 'off the planet'). Attracting
millions of tourists a year, the area was ripe for consumer
overkill, especially by makers of Millennial Outwear – air-
conditioned tents, solar-powered beach buggies, portable disco
backpacks . . . But the Elder was adamant.

'Your fibre-optic bazaar of product pushing,' he told the
magnate, seamlessly switching to Pose of the Hero, 'has turned
frugality into a dirty word and depleted the planet.'

'I've added to the planet,' said Rupert the Mighty. 'Bright
lights, big cities. You're still stuck in the twentieth century.
Most people find the bush boring.'

'Bright lights, dull brains. Of course the bush seems boring,
compared to splatter-punk. *Everything* is.' Real life seemed
duller than a test pattern. To break the grip of TV, thousands
of addicts had enrolled in twelve-step programs . . . and then
migrated to Ecotopia. 'Anyway, nature is not something you
view – nature is something you become.'

Rupert barked: 'Why go back to the stone age, like your
ancestors, the swamp galloots? Not everyone wants to roll in
the mud and eat burnt goanna.'

'Funny. That's what your doco teams wanted us to do – in
the days we were silly enough to let them in.' The Ecotopians
were trying to enlarge their psyches, the Elder said, to shift
viewpoints, to share the sensibility of other species, to be receptive to the wisdom of nature; a budding Fifth World. 'But you
see Ecotopia as one long remake of *Dot and The Kangaroo*.'

'Yeah, well, you don't do much for the GNP.'

Actually, the citizens of Ecotopia were an industrious
lot, harnessing wind, tidal and solar energy, marketing an
array of bush tucker (including Green Ant tonic and other
foodaceuticals), exporting their earth-repair skills to Asia. Fun
was high on their To Do list – white-water rafting, hang-gliding,
hanging loose, mushroom rituals.

Rupert was impatient. 'I offer power to your people. Choices. Sport, Game Shows, first run movies, even higher education.'

'The illusion of choices. It all boils down to one choice: the consumer society. Happiness equals shopping, adrenalin and cuddly toys . . .' The Elder quoted Diogenes: '"To own nothing is the beginning of happiness".' Mysteriously, his people didn't suffer the urge to own anything more than they needed. 'Ecotopians don't *want* to be a target market.'

'You're an old hippie,' Rupert said, 'Nothing beats the pleasure of work.'

'Sure – for the right objectives. But with you it's more a disease – a retreat from the existential vacuum.'

'Come again?'

'Never mind.'

'Oh, a cleaning appliance. Is it on the Shopping Channel?'

'The only way to deal with the existential vacuum is to fill it up with nature's wisdom. A time to reconnect with who you really are.'

A time to reconnect with *Baywatch*, Rupert thought, suddenly bored. He blurted: 'What a wanky indulgence. How can I deliver the outdoor market to advertisers, if everyone in Ecotopia is on a mountain getting high and gazing at their navels . . .' Phut! The Elder flicked off the monitor and beamed into the camcorder.

'If only your gaze was that high, Rupe. Here in Mabo Country, it's the stars we set our sights upon. So long . . .'

Through the earpiece came a mutter: 'If I wasn't Rupert the Mighty, I'd quite like to be the Elder from Ecotopia.'

'Surely you'd rather be both,' the minion muttered, 'high . . . *and* Mighty?'

(*Resurgence*)

Epilogue

Inside each of us, there are several voices.
Some of mine want the last say:

NORMAN NORMAL: *Pleased with yourself, huh? Your fifth book; another fifteen seconds in the spotlight, royalities, the BBC* . . .

ROMANTIC POET: *It feels strangely flat, actually.*

NORM: *Oh, come on. You just had a visit from a prominent sculptor. He flew all the way from Bermuda to take your measurements. Not many people get to be cast in bronze and put on a plinth.*

POET: *As I told him, I don't care if it's never cast.*

NORM: *In Stratford-upon-Avon, no less. So you're playing the role of the tortured artist, again. Indifferent to worldly concerns.*

THE INNER FATHER: *A bit too indifferent is what he's been.*

NORM: *Come again?*

FATHER: *Aged fifty and still scrabbling for cash. Ridiculous, don't you think?*

NORM: *But that was the whole point for him. Colourful lifestyle, shifts of consciousness — never the share market or real estate.*

POET: *I'm not so fussed about wealth, as long as the family has a cosy hearth and stuff in the fridge. It's just, well . . . I guess I'm beginning to doubt the whole role of being an outsider.*

MOTHER'S VOICE FROM THE GRAVE: *I warned you about that years ago, when you threw in a steady job for a bohemian stint at the university.*

NORM: *Exactly. It's beginning to bite, isn't it? Being an aging rebel.*

POET: *I admit to feeling ineffectual and isolated sometimes. I have an urge to warn the kids to on no account go the way I did – living on the fringe, yapping on the sidelines. As a critic once said, right at the beginning: you're a scarecrow radical – you'll frighten the sparrows for a while, and then . . . nothing. Yup. It's the same with a bronze statue, really, except that the birds cover it with shit.*

NORM: *So that magnate from Japan was right – people from the sixties will regret their entire lives.*

POET: *It's a mood thing, Norm. When my daughter bought her first peace sign, I loved it; but that soppy junior school she went to, ggrrrhhhh – all Rudolph Steiner and encounter groups; it didn't believe in homework or putting the kids under pressure – piffle. Life is tough; life is mean.*

NORM: *My, haven't we grown up? I remember the time a judge described the world as a vale of tears and you asked what he meant.*

MOTHER: *My boy caused a lot of those tears.*

POET: *We've been through that. The past is another country. Now I've shoved my daughter into a no-nonsense grammar school, where the striped tie and flannel blazer are compulsory – even during a heatwave. Okay? So what kind of hippie am I?*

MOTHER: *A hippiecrite.*

NORM: *The point is, you don't want your children to live in a wayward, fragile space, like yours.*

POET: *No. I want them to feel secure, protected, educated . . .*

*Mind you, not to put money at the centre of their beings, like
so many others.*
FATHER: *You sound less like a poet and more like me.*
POET: *It's because the very goal I didn't pursue – which
happened by chance, really – turned out to be a bulwark.
After a head-on collision in a car in Spain, other parts of my
life melted away . . . The family got closer, stronger.*
NORM: *So where to now?*
POET: *Into the next millennium, of course. Still with dreams,
a vision, a tensiled optimism, but no longer with my head stuck
in the sand.*
MOTHER: *Or in the muck. That denial of harsh reality comes
from your father's side.*
POET: *I know, I know. Right now I'm watching my uncle die
of cancer. He tells the nurses he does a hundred push-ups a day,
eats like a rhino and feels great. He believes it, too. Even the
doctors start to believe it, and send him home. My uncle fades
away on the front porch; an ambulance is called and the cycle
repeats. So I know about denial – and about the pitfalls of
'presenting well'.*
FATHER: *The funny thing is, you painted yourself into a corner
as a raving hippie, but you actually prefer to snuggle in bed with
the kids and read them stories. Even to toil over their maths.*
POET: *The last book I read – a set novel for year seven – had
the line, 'God help the children of the flower children'. I nearly
fell out of bed.*
NORM: *So now you dress up like me and fly off to soulless
convention centres in tacky resorts to tell business types about
the shape of the future. How the hell would you know?*
MOTHER: *And why should they listen – with your past?*
POET: *Actually, Mum, you'd be surprised at how many top
executives once travelled the world with* Playpower *in their*

jeans. *These days, I try to bring them fresh ideas from left field.
As I spout from the lectern: we don't know for sure what the
future may bring, but we can start to shape what we can bring to
the future. The equivalent of land, money and power in the next
century might well be our psychological health, social panache
and mind-play.*

NORM: *There you go again, sounding like a mystic know-all.*

POET: *The calamities facing the world have not, by and large,
been brought about by people like me, Norm. Okay, so I might
be on the defensive at the moment, because I probably should
have sold out and set up shop . . .*

MOTHER: *Sold out? Who'd buy you?*

POET: *. . . but the whole world can't go on grasping a bigger
share of the cake, 'cause there'll soon be no cake left. As a voice
from the wings for over thirty years, my role is to keep pumping
alternatives into the public imagination; to hasten the evolution
of bright ideas and to applaud their adoption; to admit errors;
and, most of all, to celebrate the triumphs.*

MOTHER: *The title of the book is perfect. A tribute to
mindlessness.*

POET: *It's an exalted state, according to Buddhists. If my mind
is flakey, the body is solid. They say bronze lasts 3,000 years.*

MOTHER: *Enough time for you to grow up, even.*